52 FOLLOW

DISCOVER AND DEEPEN FAITH IN JESUS

By Dan Harding

Copyright ©2024

52 *Follow: Discover and deepen faith in Jesus*
By Dan Harding

Published by Pop Strategy
Cover Design by Ellina Fletcher
Layout by Tom Carroll
Edited by Ruth Harding
Photo by @BenAndKatiePhotography

ISBN: 978-0-6486107-2-4

Unless otherwise indicated, all scripture quotations are from The ESV® Bible (The Holy Bible, English Standard Version®), © 2001 by Crossway, a publishing ministry of Good News Publishers. Used by permission. All rights reserved. Scripture quotations marked (NLT) are taken from the Holy Bible, New Living Translation, copyright © 1996, 2004, 2015 by Tyndale House Foundation. Used by permission of Tyndale House Publishers, Inc., Carol Stream, Illinois 60188. All rights reserved.

All rights reserved. No part of this publication may be reproduced, stored in a retrieval system, or transmitted in any form or by any means – for example, electronic, photocopy, recording - without the prior written permission of the publisher. The only exception is brief quotation in printed reviews.

To order more copies direct from the author please visit:
www.52follow.com

To the reader,

My hope is that you don't just discover the
teachings of Jesus, but Jesus himself.
My prayer is that you become, "fully alive",
missing out on nothing of the life that
Jesus promises to anyone who
earnestly seeks after him.

To our church,

This book is my contribution towards Jesus' call to,
"Teach these new disciples to obey all
the commands I have given you".
May we enjoy our shared life of
loving obedience to Jesus.

To my wife,

You are more like Jesus than I.
More precious to me by the day.

CONTENT

Following Jesus — 10

Going "All in" — 12

PART 1 – GOD

1. Be born again — 18
2. Repent — 22
3. Follow Me — 26
4. Worship and serve God alone — 30
5. Fear God, do not fear people — 34
6. Ask, seek, knock — 38
7. Love God with your whole self — 42
8. Abide in Jesus — 46
9. Hear + understand Jesus' words — 50
10. Give to God & Government what is rightfully theirs — 54
11. Lovingly obey Jesus — 58
12. Obey and teach God's law — 62

PART 2 – SELF

13. Don't be troubled or afraid — 68
14. Let your light shine — 72

CONTENT

15. Deny yourself ... 76
16. Rejoice and be glad ... 80
17. Do not even sin in your heart ... 84
18. Speak simply + truthfully ... 88
19. Practice righteousness in secret ... 92
20. Learn from Jesus how to rest ... 96
21. Clean the inside of the cup ... 100
22. Turn the other cheek ... 104
23. Be perfect, as your father is perfect ... 108
24. Watch + pray to avoid temptation ... 112
25. Be on your guard against all Covetousness ... 116

PART 3 – OTHERS

26. Love your neighbour as yourself ... 122
27. Invite the uninvited into your life ... 126
28. Be reconciled ... 130
29. Love your enemies ... 134
30. Judge not, that you be not judged ... 138
31. Don't replace God's commands with your traditions ... 142
32. Humble yourself like a child ... 146

33. Forgive those who sin against you ... 150

34. Do not throw your pearls to pigs ... 154

35. Do unto others... ... 158

36. Don't separate what God joins ... 162

37. Love one another as I loved you ... 166

38. Go to Christians who offend you ... 170

PART 4 – GOD'S MISSION FOR YOU

39. Seek first the kingdom of God ... 176

40. Be wise as serpents, innocent as doves ... 180

41. Shepherd other followers of Jesus ... 184

42. Ask God to send people on mission ... 188

43. Lead by being a servant ... 192

44. Choose the narrow gate ... 196

45. Remember me in the Lord's Supper ... 200

46. Make God's house a place of prayer, not profit ... 204

47. Beware of false prophets ... 208

48. Beware of false teaching + religion ... 212

49. Be prepared for my return ... 216

CONTENT

50. Lay up treasures in heaven 220
51. Go, make, baptise and teach disciples 224
52. Receive God's power for mission 228

What next? 232

Contact 235

FOLLOWING JESUS

Jesus loved life! He invited those who encountered him to not only discover true life but an entirely new way of living. To those seeking this new life, Jesus said, "Come, follow me".

This collection of 52 of Jesus' commands is offered as an echo of **Jesus' invitation to you** to, "*Come, follow me.*" This invitation wasn't simply a new moral or religious way of living. Rather, following Jesus includes an invitation into his new, ultimate experience of reality. He invites us into an intimate relationship with the true and living God. He further invites us to live, just like Him, empowered by God's Holy Spirit, with the same sense of calling and destiny that he lived. Jesus was confident that this new life would be so radically different that he described it as being "born again". This didn't mean we would return to a physical womb, but a *recreation* of our desires, dreams and capacities from scratch by God's Holy Spirit.

Each chapter of this book should stand on its own. However, together, they give us a picture of not only Jesus and his message but of ourselves and our great need for Jesus. For example, when Jesus calls us to forgive like he forgives us, we are first reminded of how merciful he is *towards us*. Secondly, we are confronted with how our own efforts to forgive others fall below even our own expectations of ourselves. Finally, as we contemplate these truths, Jesus gently teaches us that through faith in him, he not only forgives us of our *unforgiveness* but teaches us and empowers us to become someone who forgives just like he does.

Jesus' teachings have been organised into four key relationships. Firstly, Jesus teaches us how to relate to **God**. Secondly, he teaches us how to relate to **ourselves**. Thirdly, he teaches us how to relate to **people** around us. Finally, he teaches us how to embrace **God's mission** for you and I to this beautiful and broken world.

You'll notice that the assumption is that each of these relationships are *active* relationships. Jesus' commands invite us to transform how we live, move and love in this world. While some of us don't like the idea of being commanded what to do. Jesus' commands are unlike anyone else's commands. All his commands are designed to shepherd you into a life of true joy. He even describes himself as, "The way, the truth and the light"! He wants to lead you from your darkness into his light. There's no doubt his invitation is bold and if you're willing to start, then I want to affirm you for your courage!

Just like most things in life, following Jesus is best done *together*. Why not invite someone to go through this with you and share how following Jesus is challenging, growing or changing you?

Enjoy the journey!

– Dan Harding
dan@openroad.church

GOING "ALL IN"

As you learn about Jesus and seek to follow His direction it's common to get to a point where you consider going "all in", where you want to experience what he calls His *abundant life*. Consciously stepping into this new life can be understood as 'faith' - deciding that you are going to trust Him from the inside out with every part of your life. He becomes your source and your destiny, your king and your saviour, your friend and your brother. Here is a simple prayer that echoes this desire:

> Dear God,
> Please **forgive** me of my sin,
> **fill** me with your Spirit,
> and help me to **follow** Jesus with my whole life.
> Amen

If you decide to step into faith and pray this prayer or something similar then you will be blessed by God in at least three ways. You are **forgiven** by God of all your sins, you are **filled** with his Holy Spirit and you are given a new direction in life as you seek to **follow** Him completely.

Forgiven. Filled. Following.

God's forgiveness will provide not only relief from guilt and shame but also a new identity as a son or daughter in His family! God's Holy Spirit will fill you in a new and permanent way and you will begin to experience His power in both the everyday and the miraculous parts of life. This life is not only taught by Jesus but modelled by him as well! His identity was shaped by his father too! He was also filled with God's Holy Spirit at his baptism. Jesus also modelled perfect obedience to God the Father just like he calls us to. This life that he modelled for us can provide you with a new freedom. This freedom comes as you grow in understanding just how deep God's love is for you and those around you.

So as you consider the call to follow Jesus on the following pages be ready for that moment when you are ready to go 'all in' and trust Him with your whole life. When that time comes may you humbly and courageously respond with a simple and transforming faith that God has **forgiven** you, **filled** you and will help you to **follow** with your whole life.

THE PRACTICE OF FOLLOWING

If you're new to Jesus and his teachings, you don't need to feel overwhelmed! We'd encourage you to take time to learn and experiment with the simple daily practice offered below. These suggested practices have been developed by fellow Jesus followers to help you not only discover God's new truths, but a whole new way of living. This is the joy of following Jesus - learning to find your primary identity, or "self", in Jesus. The Bible describes this daily process as "putting off the old self" and "putting on the new self".

However, these daily rhythms are not just for *you*, but for you to introduce to *others*. You can help others learn from Jesus themselves, or even encourage groups of people in these rhythms together.

PRAY

Begin each time with a simple moment of prayer. At the very least, centre your mind upon Jesus. Ask God's Holy Spirit to speak to you, "Come, Holy Spirit". You may also ask for God's help in your life, the lives of loved ones or the world beyond you.

READ

Continue by discovering God's truth by reading the Bible slowly, deliberately and out loud if possible. If you're in a group, you may each want to read parts of the passage out loud together and then recount the key parts of the story together. To make the most of Jesus' teaching, you're encouraged to memorise the scripture **highlighted in bold** each week! Additional readings supplement each teaching for people who want to dig deeper throughout the rest of the week.

OBEY

Finish by reflecting upon what you read, expecting God's Holy Spirit to speak to you as you reflect on three simple questions. There are of course no "right" answers, just a willingness to listen and learn.

> **Head**: Think, *"What do I learn about God and people?"*
> **Heart**: Ask, *"God, what are you saying to me today?"*
> **Hands**: Decide, *"How will i respond to God's voice?"*

GOING DEEPER FOR GROUPS

Groups can go through this material using the simple method above. However, if the group needs more prompting or is watching accompanying videos, there are simple questions for discussion. However you utilise this resource, remember that faith in Jesus is designed to be both *lived* and *shared*! Share what you learn!

PART 1
GOD

01

BE BORN AGAIN

> READ JOHN 3:1-8
> "Now there was a man of the Pharisees named Nicodemus, a ruler of the Jews. This man came to Jesus by night and said to him, "Rabbi, we know that you are a teacher come from God, for no one can do these signs that you do unless God is with him." **Jesus answered him, "Truly, truly, I say to you, unless one is born again he cannot see the kingdom of God."**

It will be tempting for anyone reading Jesus' teachings for the first time to simply compare his words to the wisdom, philosophies or advice of other renowned thinkers, teachers and leaders of history. However, Jesus shows us right from the beginning of his season of teaching that he wasn't sent from heaven just to add a few nuggets of wisdom to the growing collection.

In John 3, Nicodemus, a respected teacher in his own right, seeks to bring Jesus down to the level of "teacher", like we are also tempted to do. See, if Jesus is simply the latest enlightened teacher to come to our attention, then we are merely upgrading our lives with the new knowledge he has for us. However, Jesus makes it clear that he didn't come to merely improve our life, enlighten our minds or offer a better religion. Rather, Jesus says he is offering us a whole new life given to us by God. Jesus describes entry into this new life as being "born again".

I've been present with my wife for seven (so far!) unique, incredible births. Not only is the physical process incredible to watch but I witnessed a child *seeing* for the first time a world they have previously only *sensed*. In the womb, we know babies can *sense* touch, sound and even light from the world outside their mother. However, it's not until the mother's body expands, contracts and breathes their child from their cocoon that they fully experience and *see* this new world.

Once born, babies begin to breathe, move, see and "live" in a completely new way. A whole new set of previously dormant instincts take over. If placed on a mother's belly moments after birth it's common for a newborn who has only been fed from the umbilical cord to instinctively crawl up to their breast and latch on for a feed as though they'd been doing it every day for nine months!

Similarly, before we have put our faith in Jesus we can sense faith, hope, life, love, beauty, courage and purpose. And yet God invites us not just to an expanded view of all that life offers, but to a completely new way of seeing. Just like a baby signals to his mother that they are ready to be born, our signal is simple - Jesus calls it faith. Upon that signal he promises to expand, contract and breathe us into not just a new life, but a whole new way of living. It's simultaneously a complete contrast to your old life as well as being the life that you instinctively knew you were always meant to be living. As you begin this journey, I would encourage you to be ready, willing and courageous to give God the signal of faith as soon as you are ready to be born again by God's Holy Spirit.

DAILY RHYTHM

PRAY
Centre your mind on Jesus. Pray, "Come, Holy Spirit".

READ
Make time to listen to or read God's Word each day.

DAY 1: John 3:1-6 *"...unless one is born again he cannot see..."*

DAY 2: 2 Cor 5:17 *"...anyone is in Christ, he is a new creation..."*

DAY 3: John 10:10 *"I came that they may have life..."*

DAY 4: Matthew 6:24 *"No one can serve two masters..."*

DAY 5: John 8:12 *"I am the light of the world..."*"

DAY 6: John 1:4 *"In him was life, and the life was...."*

DAY 7: Isaiah 43:18-19 *"...Behold, I am doing a new thing..."*

OBEY
Head: Think, *"What do I learn about God and people?"*
Heart: Ask, *"God, what are you saying to me today?"*
Hands: Decide, *"How will I respond to God's voice?"*

GOING DEEPER
* Have you ever sensed there was a new way to live?
* If you consider yourself, "Born again", what has that meant to you?

02

REPENT

> **READ MATTHEW 4:1-17**
> "*17 From that time Jesus began to preach, saying, "Repent, for the kingdom of heaven is at hand."*"

Repentance is rarely discussed today for many reasons, but most of all I think we avoid it for one key reason - *change*. Repentance is a line in the sand between the OLD and the NEW. Jesus, likewise, offers a whole NEW way of living *if* we are willing to repent, leaving our old life behind.

Jesus says the Old Testament (the part of the Bible written before Jesus) was preparing people for His coming which would usher in a whole new way of knowing and following God. This new way of knowing God is for anyone who repents of their sin. They will be forgiven and receive God's Holy Spirit to dwell in and with them forever. They then know God because he is in and with them!

But all of this starts with repentance. If you were to read

through the whole Bible you would see similar but nuanced views of repentance. Christians call the first part of their Bible the *Old Testament* and comes from the Jewish faith. These writings seem to indicate repentance is a change of direction towards God. The second part of the Bible, the *New Testament*, covers the writings of the first Christians who followed Jesus and further develops repentance as a deep, fundamental change of mind about God and the way to know him - Jesus' key message.

In the gospel of Luke (chapter 15) we read a story known as "The Prodigal Son". However, it may better be called "the Repentant Son" as this is a story of a son who has completely rejected his family, but "comes to his senses". Once the reality of life apart from his family has dawned upon him, he changes direction and seeks to humbly come home in the hopes that he'll be accepted as a servant. However, as he approaches the family farm, his father - who has been looking for his return each day - sees him and runs to greet him with overwhelming love and gratitude that his son "who was once lost has been found". Once the son encounters the love of his Father he then experiences a change of mind. He realises that his dad's love is unconditional and nothing is being held back!

This is the same journey taken by all those who come to God. We change our direction, give up forging our own road and come looking for God. However, as we seek to do this Jesus makes it clear that the repentance he is looking for requires a whole new way of thinking about God. He is not a father to reject. Nor a father who seeks to punish us for our indignities or rebellions. Our father is the one who has been waiting this whole time and has prepared the way for our return and celebration.

As you read about Jesus, read every command as an invitation to change direction and come to Him. However, he is not a taskmaster to please or a guru to impress. He is the God who has sacrificed himself so that you can experience a new life and a whole new way of knowing Him.

DAILY RHYTHM

PRAY
Centre your mind upon Jesus. Pray, "Come, Holy Spirit".

READ
Make time to read God's Word out loud each day.

DAY 1: Matthew 4:1-17 *"...Repent, for the kingdom of heaven..."*

DAY 2: Romans 2:4 *"...God's kindness is meant to lead you..."*

DAY 3: 2 Peter 3:9 *"The Lord is...patient toward you..."*

DAY 4: John 4:4-42 *"...see a man who told me everything..."*

DAY 5: Luke 19:1-10 *"Lord, the half of my goods I give..."*

DAY 6: 2 Chronicles 7:14 *"If my people who are called..."*

DAY 7: Matthew 3:8 *"Bear fruit in keeping with repentance."*

OBEY
Head: Think, *"What do I learn about God and people?"*

Heart: Ask, *"God, what are you saying to me today?"*

Hands: Decide, *"How will I respond to God's voice?"*

GOING DEEPER
* *In your own words, describe what 'repent' means?*
* *What is stopping, or has stopped, you from repenting as Jesus invites you to?*

03

FOLLOW ME

> READ MATTHEW 4:18-25
> "*¹⁹ And he said to them, "Follow me, and I will make you fishers of men."*"

Have you ever known someone who seemed to have a 'knack' for a particular task? Some kind of unique, 'miraculous' ability to do things that others find difficult? Jesus had a 'knack' for bringing thousands of people to faith in God - what he called "fishing" for people. With a genuine desire to follow Jesus, many new Christians spend their energy striving to 'win people for Jesus', commonly resulting in many failed attempts. We feel that while Jesus and a small group of super Christians have the 'knack', it's simply, "not our gift".

This frustrating experience very easily leads us to settle for a life that does not meet the expectations we once held for ourselves. While we started out with the best of intentions, our execution is where the issue lies. Unlike our old life that is totally dependent on ourselves and aimed at 'success' as a Christian; our new life of faith must be founded upon Jesus and aimed at becoming like him as the priority. In Matthew 4:19 Jesus makes it very clear that before we "fish" he wants us to "follow". In fact, at a basic level, he makes a promise to all those who've put their faith in him. He promises that *if* we are willing to follow then he will make [ensure, promise, guarantee] us into fishers of people just like him.

Anyone who has taken up a new hobby knows that no matter how many YouTube tutorials you watch, how much expensive gear you buy or how positive your mindset becomes, you can still end up looking like a fool (e.g. first-time surfing, fishing, drawing or driving). What we actually need is a coach, friend or professional who can walk alongside us, shaping us into the kind of person who makes it look effortless.

Following Jesus can be the same. Once we repent of our sin and are born again by faith we feel we are ready to *save the world*! However, like any other skill or hobby we are coached in, we must lay aside our self-assured mindset and simply and humbly follow his direction. It is in this posture of learning and worship that Jesus himself ensures that our lives will make the impact we were called and designed to have.

In striving to *fish*, many Christians fail to *follow*. If, like any humble student, you are willing to learn from Jesus step by step, it's quite likely you could develop Jesus' knack for introducing people to God without forcing him upon them.

And when you learn that, you'll know that you are well on your way to becoming like Christ himself.

DAILY RHYTHM

PRAY
Centre your mind upon Jesus. Pray, "Come, Holy Spirit".

READ
Make time to read God's Word out loud each day.

DAY 1: Matthew 4:18-25 *"Follow me, and I will make..."*

DAY 2: Luke 14:25-33 *"Whoever does not bear his own..."*

DAY 3: John 1:29-51 *"Behold, the Lamb of God, who..."*

DAY 4: John 12:20-26 *"If anyone serves me, he must..."*

DAY 5: Hebrews 12:1-6 *"...let us also lay aside every weight..."*

DAY 6: 1 Peter 2:21 *"...because Christ also suffered for you..."*

DAY 7: 1 Corinthians 11:1-2 *"Be imitators of me, as I am..."*

OBEY
Head: Think, *"What do I learn about God and people?"*
Heart: Ask, *"God, what are you saying to me today?"*
Hands: Decide, *"How will I respond to God's voice?"*

GOING DEEPER
* *Do you know someone who models Jesus well?*
* *What would it take for you to go all-in and follow Jesus with your whole life?*

04

WORSHIP AND SERVE GOD ALONE

> **READ LUKE 4:1-15**
> "*⁸ And Jesus answered him, "It is written, "'You shall worship the Lord your God, and him only shall you serve.'"*"

What are you like when you're hungry? Do you get agitated, distracted, grumpy, lazy? Whatever your version of hunger-affected life is, you probably aren't at your best. We often say that when we are hungry we have a "one-track mind"; we just want to eat! Knowing that Jesus experienced all the human limitations that we all feel, Satan tempted Jesus when he was at his weakest - alone and hungry. If Jesus would give up on worship and obedience to God, then Satan promised to meet his needs. Of course, this was an empty promise as Satan cannot provide anything that Jesus, or we, truly need.

It's no surprise that temptation came in a moment of need.

While many of our greatest needs, such as food and companionship, are valid, none of them are to supersede our worship and obedience to God. For Jesus, worship is really an assessment of our true and deepest feelings about God - our *appetite* for Him. To relate our spiritual health with our affections is not as far-fetched as it may first seem! The truth is that our affections in life set our direction in life. If we love fitness we become fit. If we love God (worship) we become like Jesus, his son. **Affection sets direction.** Worship is thus like a spiritual GPS. As we continually affirm our love for God as our ultimate desire we find our lives aligning with God's purposes, not our own.

How do we cultivate this kind of affection for God, a life that unwaveringly worships and serves God over all others? To continue the food analogy, some of us may need to go on a diet. Not a food-based diet, but a spiritual diet. See, the healthiest form of dieting is not simply losing weight, but growing a new appetite. Where we used to crave physical foods that are low in nutrition and energy, we ideally discover and grow an appetite for highly nutritious foods that fuel our bodies. Spiritually, we might examine our own lives and remove any activities or desires that provide low spiritual nourishment. In their place, we focus on growing an appetite for activities or desires that meet our deepest spiritual longings and needs. This could include prayer, reading, memorising or meditating on scripture, serving the poor, opening up our lives or fasting.

Leading up to his temptation in the wilderness, Jesus was

fasting. He wasn't simply depriving himself of food, but deepening his love for God. Like Jesus, learning how to fast in a healthy manner deepens our affection for God. Instead of spending our days identifying and filling our bodily needs, fasting identifies and fills our spiritual needs. This is the journey Jesus walked out in Luke. After overcoming Satan's temptation and maintaining his affection for God he left the wilderness, "in the power of the Spirit" and continued to live out God's purpose for his life. To fulfil the purposes God has for *you*, cultivate an affection for God that is stronger than the temptations to a lesser path in life. Affections set direction.

DAILY RHYTHM

PRAY
Centre your mind upon Jesus. Pray, "Come, Holy Spirit".

READ
Make time to read God's Word out loud each day.

DAY 1: Luke 4:1-15 *"...You shall worship the Lord your God..."*
DAY 2: Matthew 13: 1–9, 18–23 *"...sown on good soil..."*
DAY 3: Joshua 24:14-15 *"...choose this day whom you will..."*
DAY 4: Luke 10:38-42 *"Martha, Martha, you are anxious..."*
DAY 5: Mark 10:35-45 *"...Son of Man came not to be served..."*
DAY 6: Luke 6:43-45 *"...out of the abundance of the heart..."*
DAY 7: John 21:15-19 *"Simon, son of John, do you love me?"*

OBEY
Head: Think, *"What do I learn about God and people?"*
Heart: Ask, *"God, what are you saying to me today?"*
Hands: Decide, *"How will I respond to God's voice?"*

GOING DEEPER
* Write out a list of who or what has your affections in life.
* How might your direction in life change if your affections were re-oriented on God?

05

FEAR GOD, DO NOT FEAR PEOPLE

> READ LUKE 12:1-14
> "⁴ I tell you, my friends, **do not fear those who kill the body, and after that have nothing more that they can do.** ⁵ But I will warn you whom to fear: fear him who, after he has killed, has authority to cast into hell. Yes, I tell you, fear him!"

Jesus' command on fear is easily misunderstood by his followers, especially given that he begins by saying, "Don't fear...", then, "Be afraid, be VERY afraid" (verses 4-5). This can challenge our expectations of Jesus, the one we thought was here to bring "good news". Furthermore, we are often unaware of the place that fear has in the frailness of our human nature.

At the beginning of Luke chapter 12, we see that the people pursuing Jesus were experiencing FOMO (Fear Of Missing

Out). No one wanted to miss out on *their* encounter with Jesus. They were so desperate to see him themselves, that they were trampling each other! Fear had taken over their better judgement and natural concern for those around them. This is likely due to some Jewish religious leaders (Pharisees) having an oppressive, intimidating control over the Jewish people. Some were living in such fear that they had to either keep their real feelings to themselves or privately whisper them to each other (verses 2-3). They were not free to follow their conscience or God in the way they saw fit. Their lives were controlled by fear!

We know that this kind of *ungodly fear* isn't the fear Jesus wants for us. It diminishes our humanity and makes us less than who we've been designed to be. This kind of ungodly fear seeks to control you and me to the point that we lose our *self-control*, threatening ourselves and others.

In contrast, Jesus is inviting us into what we might term a *godly fear*. Fearing God himself might sound like merely replacing one terror for another, but the reality is far from it. Your greatest fear in life will have the greatest influence on your life. In fact, for some, their greatest fear becomes like a god to them. This is why we fear God and not men or women. We want God to drive the purpose and destiny for our lives, not those who seek to diminish and destroy our future. When we fear God we become more of who we're designed to be. We begin to grow into people who are not controlled by fear but begin to exude self-control. When we fear God, we come to realise that God's infinite power is far greater than any man or woman who seeks to control us. We then gain a godly perspective on fear, fearing only whom we should, not those we shouldn't.

This is like a child who is afraid of the dark. Rather than telling them, "There's nothing to be afraid of", we simply bring the presence of a greater power - mum, dad or another loved one - into their room. They then become assured that if mum or dad are there then they don't need to be afraid of the monsters because mum and dad are more powerful! Likewise, Jesus wants us to live without fear of anyone else who seeks to control our lives. God *is* greater, and by fearing him we are set free from every other power and fear that we might enjoy true freedom.

DAILY RHYTHM

PRAY
Centre your mind upon Jesus. Pray, "Come, Holy Spirit".

READ
Make time to read God's Word out loud each day.

DAY 1: Luke 12:1-14 "...do not fear those who kill..."

DAY 2: John 14:15-31 *"Peace I leave with you; my peace..."*

DAY 3: Isaiah 41:8-10 *"...fear not, for I am with you;"*

DAY 4: Joshua 1:1-9 *"Be strong and courageous."*

DAY 5: Psalm 56:1-4 *"When I am afraid, I put my trust..."*

DAY 6: Roman 1:16-17 *"For I am not ashamed of the gospel..."*

DAY 7: John 20:19-23 *"[Jesus] said..., "Peace be with you."*

OBEY
Head: Think, *"What do I learn about God and people?"*
Heart: Ask, *"God, what are you saying to me today?"*
Hands: Decide, *"How will I respond to God's voice?"*

GOING DEEPER
* *Do you have any ungodly fears in your life?*
* *How might godly fear bring you freedom from this ungodly fear?*

06

ASK, SEEK, KNOCK

READ MATTHEW 7:7-11
"⁷ *"Ask, and it will be given to you; seek, and you will find; knock, and it will be opened to you.* ⁸ *For everyone who asks receives, and the one who seeks finds, and to the one who knocks it will be opened..."*

Have you ever been courageous enough to boldly ask God for something from the bottom of your heart? If so, it's quite likely that it was in a season of desperation when it seemed like there was nowhere else to turn. While this is wonderful, it's not the picture Jesus is trying to paint as the normal, everyday way to pray. Jesus invites us to ask God for whatever it is we need, *whenever* we need it.

One of the simple reasons some of us fail to send our requests to God is that we can be too quick to question either our intentions or his. This is because the more we know Jesus the more we realise our faults and ill-intentions that lurk deep within us. This can make us too quick to silence the desires that arise within us each day. Likewise, much of our culture questions whether God really wants to meet our needs. Many even question, "Is he even listening anyway?"

In contrast to our cautions, Jesus simply says, "Ask, seek, knock! Got a prayer? Pray! Looking for answers? Explore! Want a new direction? Step!" It seems that he is encouraging us to throw our cautions and concerns to the wind and entrust ourselves and our mixed bag of intentions to God. One of the reasons Jesus seems so confident to encourage us to simply reach for what we want is that he knows that our Father in Heaven isn't going to give us anything evil. Neither is he simply required to give us exactly what we ask for either! In fact, aside from not giving us stones or snakes for food, his fatherly nature is to give us *surprisingly good* gifts.

If I ask my kids what they want for breakfast they may say, "Ice cream"! In response, I'd never give them gravel, but neither would I necessarily give them ice cream. While their desire is for ice cream, they are simply immaturely expressing their need for sustenance. So I might respond with a *good, healthy* answer to their request, "How about eggs on toast? Or honey and pancakes?" I'm doing what a good father aims to do, to meet the needs of my children with as much lovingkindness as I can. On the weekends I may even suggest, "Hey, how about pancakes *with* ice cream?!" The reason I'd add in the ice cream is simply because I am filled with joy when I meet not only their *needs* but also their *desires*.

Once we realise that God *is* good and only brings good answers to our requests, we won't fear our own ill-intent or God's malicious response. Rather, we become like a little child with a father who loves to cook for them! We simply ask, "Please God can I have some......?". So, ask. Seek. Knock.

DAILY RHYTHM

PRAY
Centre your mind upon Jesus. Pray, "Come, Holy Spirit".

READ
Make time to read God's Word out loud each day.

DAY 1: Matthew 7:7-11 *"...Ask, and it will be given to you..."*

DAY 2: John 16:24 *"Ask, and you will receive...."*

DAY 3: James 4:3, 5:16 *"...because you ask wrongly,..."*

DAY 4: Matt 21:18-22 *"...you will receive, if you have faith"*

DAY 5: Psalm 66:16-20 *"...[God] has attended to the voice..."*

DAY 6: Romans 8:31-38 *"...graciously give us all things?"*

DAY 7: 1 John 3:19-24 *"...we receive from him..."*

OBEY
Head: Think, *"What do I learn about God and people?"*
Heart: Ask, *"God, what are you saying to me today?"*
Hands: Decide, *"How will I respond to God's voice?"*

GOING DEEPER
* *Do you find it easy to believe that God desires to give you good gifts?*

* *Is there a need in your life that you can ask God to meet?*

07

LOVE GOD WITH YOUR WHOLE SELF

> READ MATTHEW 22:34-40
>
> "*³⁷ And he said to him, "You shall love the Lord your God with all your heart and with all your soul and with all your mind. This is the great and first commandment. And a second is like it: You shall love your neighbour as yourself. On these two commandments depend all the Law and the Prophets."*

Jesus breaks down the entire Judeo-Christian commandments by guiding us to love UP (love God) and love OUT (love those around us). Rather than being simplistic and childish, Jesus offers a profoundly fresh perspective on what it means to live the life we were designed for.

While both commands are well-known, the *first* commandment to love God with your heart, soul and mind often plays second fiddle to the *second* commandment. This may be because it's less practical and sometimes hard to measure or define. When you love others, people notice, but when you love God, you're the only one who can be sure of what's happening within yourself.

However, my suspicion is that we overlook the depths of this commandment because it challenges our core beliefs about ourselves. We prefer to assume that our heart's intentions are good, our soul is pure and our mind typically arrives at good conclusions. We so easily say, "Of course I love God". And yet Jesus is reminding us that in fact, all of us see evidence of different loves rising and falling in our heart, soul and mind.

The reality is that for many of us, unless we follow Jesus' command to intentionally love UP, our love easily drifts to whatever, or whomever, we are surrounded by: "I love my job", "I love my spouse", "I love cars", "I love food"! As good as work, romance, cars and food are, if we are not intentionally directing our heart UP, it becomes enraptured by whatever and whoever we are surrounded by. These people and things, rather than God, then dictate the direction and flavour of our lives. This is why this commandment is the first and primary commandment. Jesus speaks directly to the core of our being, inviting us to align our deepest loves with God himself so that this love might shape every detail and direction of our lives.

All that we will ever visibly *do* for God in this life, comes out of this simple mandate to love *God first*. The challenge is not to love God more than other people appear to but to offer as much of our heart, soul and mind as we are able. As any newlywed or parent has experienced, the sensational "honeymoon phase" does fade, but in its place, we have the opportunity to cultivate a richer love by offering new parts of our our heart, soul and mind to our loved ones.

Similarly, we should learn to love God just as we started out, going 'all in'. In this way, we never compare ourselves with others, or consider ourselves "not good enough". We simply love God with every part of ourselves that we have to offer. What part of your life are you yet to give to God?

DAILY RHYTHM

PRAY
Centre your mind upon Jesus. Pray, "Come, Holy Spirit".

READ
Make time to read God's Word out loud each day.

DAY 1: Matthew 22:34-40 *"...You shall love the Lord..."*

DAY 2: John 14:15-21 *"If you love me, you will keep..."*

DAY 3: Romans 6:1-14 *"Present yourselves to God..."*

DAY 4: Galatians 2:20 *"It is no longer I who live, but..."*

DAY 5: Prov 16:1-9 *"Commit your work to the Lord..."*

DAY 6: Hebrews 13:16 *"Do not neglect to do good..."*

DAY 7: Romans 5:1-5 *"...we have peace with God..."*

OBEY
Head: Think, *"What do I learn about God and people?"*

Heart: Ask, *"God, what are you saying to me today?"*

Hands: Decide, *"How will I respond to God's voice?"*

GOING DEEPER
* Who or what have you prioritised in the past year?
* What might it look like for you to love God above everything else?

08

ABIDE IN JESUS

> READ JOHN 15:1-17
> *"...Abide in me, and I in you. As the branch cannot bear fruit by itself, unless it abides in the vine, neither can you, unless you abide in me..."*

Our culture rewards people who appear to have become independently successful. People who seem to have "made something of their life" without the undue influence of parents, employers, partners or friends. People who can proudly "stand on their own two feet". Even in a moral and spiritual sense many in our day feel compelled - and even encouraged - to create their own morality or spirituality. We feel justified to "live our own truth". Even followers of Jesus like you and I can unintentionally adopt this mindset. We unwittingly make selective use of his teachings for our gain. Or we use Jesus' words to justify going off in our own direction, yet still expect to produce ("bear") what the Bible calls healthy spiritual "fruit" (see Galatians 5:22-23).

Jesus makes it clear that His plan for you is different. His path is not simply a "better" path than your previous one, but a different path that you walk together with Him. He wants to journey so closely entwined that you grow fruit by association, not merely performance. This is not an exclusively spiritual or religious model of life. We see this model of growth at work in families when children learn by imitating their parents - using toy hammers, mixers and computers to emulate those they look up to. It's not just children who learn this way. Apprentices learn from tradespeople. Athletes learn from coaches. Students learn from tutors. Juniors learn from seniors.

One of the keys in these relationships is being close enough to pick up the subtle tips, nuanced movements that our teachers do intuitively. Jesus says in John chapter 15 that we are to similarly pay close attention to his "words" and "commandments" as he has paid attention to His Father's. Without minimising the supernatural dynamics in following Jesus, Jesus reveals that the simplest way to abide in him is to simply learn from his person and teaching. Love how he loves. Think how he thinks. Serve how he serves. Give how he gives. Pray how he prays. This can only happen when we are close enough to *abide* in him.

Jesus view his followers as a branch that cannot survive without its vine. In fact, a branch makes no sense and has no purpose without a vine! Similarly, Jesus invites us to discover our purpose and identity in reference to him, our vine. In everyday terms, we should thus gravitate towards activities, thoughts and people that draw us into this abiding relationship and avoid ones that do not! For some, it's exploring prayer and daily Bible reading, or beginning to attend a local church.

While Jesus' example of abiding with His Father required great sacrifice and discipline, he clearly believes that this kind of life is *full* of joy! It seems that the life we most earnestly seek is the life that's lived most intimately with him. So, learn to abide in Jesus so that your life might truly thrive.

DAILY RHYTHM

PRAY
Centre your mind upon Jesus. Pray, "Come, Holy Spirit".

READ
Make time to read God's Word out loud each day.

DAY 1: John 15:1-17 *"...Abide in me, and I in you"*

DAY 2: Matt 11:28 *"Come to me all who are weary..."*

DAY 3: 1 Jn 4:16 *"...whoever abides in love abides in God..."*

DAY 4: 1 Jn 4:12 *"...if we love one another, God abides in us..."*

DAY 5: 1 Jn 2:6 *"Whoever says he abides in him ought to..."*

DAY 6: Gal 2:20 *"It is no longer I who live, but Christ..."*

DAY 7: 2 Cor 12:9 *"My grace is sufficient for you..."*

OBEY
Head: Think, *"What do I learn about God and people?"*
Heart: Ask, *"God, what are you saying to me today?"*
Hands: Decide, *"How will I respond to God's voice?"*

GOING DEEPER
* *Do you feel like you have to prove yourself to others?*
* *If abiding in Jesus is fundamental to your new life, what would healthy markers of success look like for you?*

09

HEAR + UNDERSTAND JESUS' WORDS

READ MATTHEW 13:1-23
"*⁹ He who has ears, let him hear.*"

Whether you're someone who is simply interested in Jesus or someone who has gone "all-in", his very blunt, "he who has ears, let him hear", may even seem a tad insulting. *Of course,* we would be hanging off every word Jesus says, right? However, the *hearing* that Jesus is talking about is not simply processing the voice of Jesus in our minds. Rather, it's the second part of a three-part process that he outlines in the 15th verse of chapter 13. He observes that the Israelites (the ancient people that God chose to work through to bring His purposes into the world), his disciples and now we have all been given the opportunity to 'see', 'hear' and finally 'understand' God and His word. But, we may ask, "If there are three parts, why is Jesus highlighting 'hearing'"?

Like the wisdom that parents, mentors, coaches and

teachers attempt to impart, our lives are full of moments and seasons where we wilfully ignore God's directives for our lives. The simplest way to ignore God is willful disobedience, "God, I know I'm not meant to steal this money, but I'm stealing it anyway". The more sophisticated strategy (or so we tell ourselves) is to pretend that we hadn't even *heard* God's directions at all. When God spoke to us his words simply went, "in one ear, and out the other". We *heard* nothing. This strategy justifies our disobedience by declaring not simply that "I don't understand *why* I shouldn't lust after another person's spouse?", but by declaring to God that, "You never even *told* me it was wrong to lust!" It's very similar to the original act of sin recorded in Genesis - we all look for reasons to justify why *our rebellion* isn't *our fault.*

In our grandparents' era, many children were told, "Children should be seen and not heard". This was a convenient way of distancing parents and carers from having to engage with the children they were responsible for. If they had to engage with their questions or requests ("hearing" them), then they would have to spend time *understanding* them and acting in a responsible fashion. It was much simpler to simply *see* children but ignore everything they had to say and thus avoid the obligation to respond to requests that might inconvenience the life of a preoccupied adult.

There will come a time for all followers of Jesus when it's much easier to treat Jesus like a 19th-century child. He should be, "seen and not heard". We might acknowledge his presence, or even that we belong to the same family. However, we avoid fully engaging with his commands lest they call into question our comfortable, preoccupied, self-focused lives. Jesus' teachings are designed to be much more than meaningless mantras, artwork on our walls or bumper stickers on our cars. He and His teachings are to be seen, *heard* and *understood*, so that we might lovingly obey him in all things. It's this kind of holistic life of faith that Jesus says will yield a "crop" - a fruitful life - that is 30, 60 and 100-fold what is expected from a life lived otherwise. So, go, be fruitful and truly live!

DAILY RHYTHM

PRAY
Centre your mind upon Jesus. Pray, "Come, Holy Spirit".

READ
Make time to read God's Word out loud each day.

DAY 1: Matthew 13:1-23 *"He who has ears, let him hear."*

DAY 2: Matthew 7:24-27 *"...who hears these words of mine..."*

DAY 3: 2 Corinthians 10:1-6 *"...take every thought captive..."*

DAY 4: 1 Samuel 15:22 *"...to obey is better than sacrifice..."*

DAY 5: Luke 11:28 *"Blessed rather are those who hear..."*

DAY 6: 1 Peter 1:14 *"...do not be conformed to the passions..."*

DAY 7: Acts 17:10-11 *"...examining the Scriptures daily..."*

OBEY
Head: Think, *"What do I learn about God and people?"*
Heart: Ask, *"God, what are you saying to me today?"*
Hands: Decide, *"How will I respond to God's voice?"*

GOING DEEPER
* Do you consistently ignore God in any area of your life?
* What has God been saying to you recently that you need to hear, understand and obey?

10

GIVE TO GOD & GOVERNMENT WHAT IS RIGHTFULLY THEIRS

> READ MATTHEW 22:1-22
> "...Then he said to them, 'Therefore **render to Caesar the things that are Caesar's, and to God the things that are God's.'.."

Similar to Jesus' day, our modern, Western culture has strong opinions on the power battles between religious and state institutions - what we often discuss today as the "separation of church and state". Rather than taking sides in this hot topic of "religion and politics", Jesus injects a nuanced perspective that elevates neither religious institutions nor the state, but God himself.

After a parable about not letting earthly responsibilities diminish our responsibility to God, the religious leaders sought to trap Jesus by forcing him to accept or reject the authority of their ruling, Roman oppressors. Critical to the context of this encounter is that the Roman emperor, Caesar, considered himself divine and had imprinted his likeness on the currency (i.e. a denarius coin) in which the Jewish people were required to pay taxes. In effect, this required Jewish people to hold and spend Roman currency that depicted Caesar as the divine authority over them. Therefore, if Jesus replied, "Yes, you should pay taxes to Caesar", he could be shown to be a heretic for accepting Caesar's authority over God's. If he said "No, don't pay taxes", he would be seen as a dangerous revolutionary seeking to overthrow the ruling authorities of the day.

However, Jesus begins to turn the tables upon his accusers and reveals their hypocrisy by asking them, "Whose likeness" is on the coins required to pay tax? The answer is obvious; Caesar's image is on the denarius because it's Caesar's own, self-created *fiat* currency. Therefore, why wouldn't Jesus permit the paying of a tax to the person who created the currency themselves?

In teaching that the "likeness", or *image*, of someone identifies ownership, the leaders would have their sacred creation story roaring in their minds. God said at creation that he made every man and woman in *the imago dei* - the image of God. If the same logic of currency applies, then wouldn't our very lives belong to God himself? If he created us all and placed *his* divine image on us, then no matter what currency any earthly ruler demanded of us, the entirety of our being should be given over to his holy authority.

Jesus thus affirms that Christian submission to God's authority should foster submission to the earthly authorities that he permits (civil, church and family). Any citizen of heaven should thus aim to be a faithful citizen on earth. However, Jesus also has a plan for transforming everyone and everything in the world. He seems to indicate that the greatest challenge to world peace is not simply a corrupt, unjust system, but *ourselves*. His command to respect the authorities around us is as much an invitation to overthrow the government we most often resist, our own unruly *self-government*. After all, as Jesus has illustrated, we are made in God's image and designed to be subject to his authority, more so than any currency or political power.

DAILY RHYTHM

PRAY
Centre your mind upon Jesus. Pray, "Come, Holy Spirit".

READ
Make time to read God's Word out loud each day.

DAY 1: Matt 22:1-32 *"...render to Caesar the things..."*

DAY 2: Rom 12:1 *"...present your bodies as a living sacrifice..."*

DAY 3: Rom 13:1-7 *"...be subject to the governing authorities."*

DAY 4: Exodus 20:12, Ephesians 6:1-4 *"Honour your..."*

DAY 5: Jeremiah 29:7 *"Seek the welfare of the city...."*

DAY 6: 1 Thessalonians 5:12 *"Respect those who labour..."*

DAY 7: Luke 2:41-52 *"Jesus...was submissive to them."*

OBEY
Head: Think, *"What do I learn about God and people?"*
Heart: Ask, *"God, what are you saying to me today?"*
Hands: Decide, *"How will I respond to God's voice?"*

GOING DEEPER
* To which authority (e.g. government, school, church, work, family) do you find it hardest to show respect?

* Do you live as though you're "under" God's authority?

11

LOVINGLY OBEY JESUS

> READ JOHN 14:1-24
> "*15...If you love me, you will keep my commandments...*"

In theory, an all-powerful God shouldn't need to offer incentives for obedience to his commands, especially if they are so good for us. However, Jesus presents a compelling and intimate case for delighting the God who created us.

When it comes to the outcomes of our obedience, Jesus makes his loving intentions clear. Jesus says in verse 23 that he and his father will make their "home with" those who "love" him and "keep" His words - those who lovingly obey him. This image of sharing a house or family with Jesus and His Father gives us the perfect analogy for imagining the intersection of love and obedience.

In any family household or relationship, there is tension between loving feelings and loving actions. Most children grow up loving their parents but then are rudely shocked when, at some point in their development towards adulthood, they are given 'chores'. They begin to wonder, "How is it that the person we experienced such pure love with now expects us to do work for them?" At some point in that development process we begin to pitch in around the house regardless of how we feel towards our parent(s). We then see the benefit of working together in love. Not only does the household thrive, but we strengthen and reflect the values of the ideal family within which we exist.

The ideal scenario in each household is that we fulfil our jobs not just because they are necessary (washing up, vacuuming, mowing) but because we joyfully fulfil our roles out of pure love. This is not only great for us, but the very thing that God himself seeks - a family that acts out of, and for, love. It's what we could term *loving* obedience.

It's not simply 'better' to have a God that asks for loving, rather than blind, obedience. Obedience that is simply 'ticking the box' may produce some positive outcomes, but it falls far short of the compelling, abundant life that Jesus invites us to. This is why Jesus invites us to a faith that is beyond mere subservience to a superior being.

The faith that Jesus aspires for all of us is a faith guided by loving obedience to a loving, and powerful, Father God. To lovingly obey Jesus is to participate in the ideal household, securely loved by our heavenly father and lovingly obedient to him in return.

DAILY RHYTHM

PRAY
Centre your mind upon Jesus. Pray, "Come, Holy Spirit".

READ
Make time to read God's Word out loud each day.

DAY 1: John 14:1-23 *"I am the way and the truth and the life."*

DAY 2: Hebrews 5:8-9 *"...was a son, he learned obedience..."*

DAY 3: John 1:1-18 *"In him was life and this life was the..."*

DAY 4: John 6:68-69 *"You have the words of eternal life."*

DAY 5: John 7:38 *"...heart will flow rivers of living water."*

DAY 6: Revelation 3:14-22 *"I discipline those whom I love."*

DAY 7: 1 John 5:3 *"...His commandments are not burdensome..."*

OBEY
Head: Think, *"What do I learn about God and people?"*
Heart: Ask, *"God, what are you saying to me today?"*
Hands: Decide, *"How will I respond to God's voice?"*

GOING DEEPER
* Do you enjoy doing what you're told?
* Since obedience is loving Jesus, what difficult command that you've ignored or overlooked could you revisit?

12

OBEY AND TEACH GOD'S LAW

READ MATT 5:1-20

"*[17] Do not think that I have come to abolish the Law or the Prophets; I have not come to abolish them but to fulfil them...[19] Therefore whoever relaxes one of the least of these commandments and teaches others to do the same will be called least in the kingdom of heaven, but whoever does them and teaches them will be called great in the kingdom of heaven.*"

The Bible is separated into two broad sections, known as the Old and New Testaments. Pre-Jesus, the Old Testament outlined the story of God's interactions with the people of Israel, especially his shaping of their nation via his Law and the words of his prophets. Because many modern readers of Jesus have a modern, individualistic worldview, his teaching on the "Law" and "the Prophets" can be misunderstood or diminished in at least two ways. Firstly, some mistakenly believe he was trashing God's old laws in favour of his new, *love-based* approach. Secondly, and in contrast to the first misunderstanding, some imply that obeying the old laws is still necessary to get your "ticket to heaven". Jesus' teaching in Matthew chapter 5 clears that up.

Those with the first misunderstanding need to know that Christ wasn't trying to "boil *down*" God's law, but rather to "sum it *up*". Jesus wasn't aiming to diminish God's original laws but to affirm and crown them. In fact, rather than replacing God's laws, he encapsulates, or fulfils, all of God's truth in one actionable word - love. Jesus isn't creating a longer list of religious laws, but fulfilling and perfecting them, showing us what they look like, "in the flesh".

Imagine you had been diligently saving and investing for many years to buy a home. On the day you finalise the loan you learn your Great Aunt passed and left you an inheritance so large you'll never have to work again! While you could cast your wise habits aside, wisdom would encourage you to continue saving and investing despite your financial windfall! Likewise, just because our sins are forgiven through Christ, and he has revealed that a heart of love for God and others is the ultimate goal, the truth, beauty and wisdom of God's ancient laws remain!

The second misunderstanding arises, in part, because we misunderstand the point of this teaching. Jesus' present point isn't how you enter heaven, this is clearly by *faith* in Jesus, not personal performance or morality. Rather, Jesus is making it clear that there will be recognition in heaven for those who obey both him and the laws he came to fulfil. Obedience to the old laws doesn't give you a *ticket* to heaven, but *rewards* when you arrive there, by faith.

In Jesus, we gain a deeper understanding of God, his laws and the life they're designed for. If Jesus and his life of love are the sum of God's law, then we need to treasure it not to *become* righteous, but to become like Jesus, the only perfect human and the one who *makes us* righteous. Have you put your faith in Jesus? Learn from him to embody God's ancient laws in a life of true love for God and those around you.

DAILY RHYTHM

PRAY
Centre your mind upon Jesus. Pray, "Come, Holy Spirit".

READ
Make time to read God's Word out loud each day.

DAY 1: Matt 5:17-19 *"Whoever does them and teaches them..."*
DAY 2: Deuteronomy 6:4-7 *"You shall teach them diligently..."*
DAY 3: Romans 7:1-12, 8:1-8 *"...what the law...could not do."*
DAY 4: Romans 13:8-14 *"...love is the fulfilling of the law."*
DAY 5: Galatians 5:10-22 *"Is the law then contrary..."*
DAY 6: Galatians 5:23-29 *"...law was our guardian until..."*
DAY 7: John 1:14-20 *"...grace and truth came through Jesus..."*

OBEY
Head: Think, *"What do I learn about God and people?"*
Heart: Ask, *"God, what are you saying to me today?"*
Hands: Decide, *"How will I respond to God's voice?"*

GOING DEEPER
* What "laws" are most valuable to your community?
* Does the gift of Jesus offer new light on any of God's old laws or Christian traditions you are aware of?

PART 2
SELF

13

DON'T BE TROUBLED OR AFRAID

> READ JOHN 14:15-31
> [27] *"Peace I leave with you; my peace I give to you. Not as the world gives do I give to you. Let not your hearts be troubled, neither let them be afraid."*

Every one of us has unique troubles and fears. For some, it's the pace of change and uncertainty, while for others it's health challenges, financial hurdles or family disunity.

Yet even when our day-to-day circumstances are stable, fear of what could potentially go wrong in the future can still cripple some of us. Though we live in the most prosperous, secure and peaceful time in history, society is more anxious and stressed than ever. Fear can crush individuals and families and deep down we all know, "Life isn't meant to be like this!"

Jesus agrees. He desires our world to be in peace, not chaos.

However, in John 14:27 Jesus doesn't give his attention to the troubles and fears that we are so easily distracted by. Rather, Jesus put his attention on - and now calls our attention to - our hearts.

If we had it our way we'd probably ask God for magical powers to banish all external troubles and hardships from our lives. However, Jesus gives us a greater challenge, the challenge to see internal transformation in our hearts - the very centre of our being.

Jesus says in John chapter 14 that he accomplishes this internal heart transformation through the presence and power of his Holy Spirit. He gives us his Holy Spirit when we put our faith in Him. And it's his Holy Spirit's presence in our life that brings us peace. This is why every one of us who follows Jesus in faith can have peace amidst any trouble or fear.

Jesus is offering us an entirely new strategy to address fear in our lives. Simply trying to minimise the troubles and fears *around* us isn't enough. Rather, we need to take moments each day to appreciate God's presence and peace *within* us.

This is more than just a private gift for you and I. God's peace is a powerful gift that, if treasured well, will begin to ripple out to calm the troubles and fears of the world around us.

Today, why don't you experiment with treasuring God's peaceful presence in your life? You might consider a simple prayer (written, spoken or thought) thanking God for his presence or slowly read Psalm 16 or 84 and then meditate on what it might mean for you personally. If God highlights part of these psalms (or any other scripture about his presence), you could write it out and stick it on your wall, fridge or mirror! Some people write calendar notes or reminders on their phones so that at key moments in each day, they are reminded that, "God's presence is within them!"

DAILY RHYTHM

PRAY
Centre your mind upon Jesus. Pray, "Come, Holy Spirit".

READ
Make time to read God's Word out loud each day.

DAY 1: Luke 12:1-17 *"...But I will warn you whom to fear..."*

DAY 2: John 20:19-23 *"Jesus came and stood among them...."*

DAY 3: Colossians 3:15-17 *"And let the peace of Christ rule..."*

DAY 4: Philippians 4:4-7 *"And the peace of God..."*

DAY 5: Galatians 5:22-23 *"But the fruit of the Spirit is love..."*

DAY 6: Isaiah 26:1-4 *"You keep him in perfect peace..."*

DAY 7: Acts 4:23-31 *"Lord, look upon their threats..."*

OBEY
Head: Think, "What do I learn about God and people?"
Heart: Ask, "God, what are you saying to me today?"
Hands: Decide, "How will I respond to God's voice?"

GOING DEEPER
* *In what situation(s) do you feel most afraid?*
* *Who did Jesus leave with us and how could his presence change your fears in the future?*

14

LET YOUR LIGHT SHINE

> **READ MATTHEW 5:1-16**
> "*[14] You are the light of the world. A city set on a hill cannot be hidden. [15] Nor do people light a lamp and put it under a basket, but on a stand, and it gives light to all in the house. [16] In the same way, **let your light shine before others, so that they may see your good works and give glory to your Father who is in heaven.**"*

In today's Christian culture we often talk about God as "light" and at Christmas we have many carols about how Jesus is the "light of the world". So when we hear Jesus say in Matthew 5 verses 13 and 14 that those who follow Him are the "salt of the earth" and the "light of the world" it raises some questions! If *he* is the light, how can *we* also be light?

Jesus assures us that since His followers are forgiven and filled with his Holy Spirit their lives have a new capacity to shine! In this scripture, he says this shining is expressed in good works - acts of love, generosity and compassion. Yet these good works are not done in order to draw attention to ourselves and show how good we are. Rather, in Jesus' mind, the kind of life that shines is the one that shows *how good God is*. The goal isn't to simply be "good" *people*, but to reveal the goodness of *God*!

Every day we rub shoulders with people in streets, beaches, parks and workplaces who sense the world's darkness and are looking for God's light! Many are awaiting a light to shine on them and say, "Yes! God is real. He *sees* you. He *is good* and *he loves you*." This is why Jesus says to let our lights shine. It's for His glory and the good of those around us.

Despite the great need for light, there's no need to be overwhelmed that it's all up to us. While together, Jesus calls us, "a city on a hill", Jesus directs each of us to simply light up our own 'house' (Matthew 5:15). In the same way each house has unique lighting based on its size, style and occupants, the people we live, work, study and play with need God's light shone in unique ways. While I cannot share Jesus with the people I work with, I can share Jesus with those I live with. While you cannot reveal God's goodness to those on the other side of the world, you can share it with those on your own street. It just might be that God has put you in your current family, workplace, team or neighbourhood so that your experience, language, relationships, education, mindset or disposition can shine Jesus in a uniquely effective manner!

If we each light up the "houses" God places us in, together

we will become the "city on a hill" that can light up the entire world! So what kind of light has God given you and to whom can *you* most easily shine? Are there people in your home, neighbourhood, workplace or friendship circle that God has positioned you to share God's goodness with?

DAILY RHYTHM

PRAY
Centre your mind upon Jesus. Pray, "Come, Holy Spirit".

READ
Make time to read God's Word out loud each day.

DAY 1: Matthew 5:13-16 *"Let your light shine before others..."*
DAY 2: Luke 11:33-36 *"No one after lighting a lamp puts..."*
DAY 3: Ephesians 2:1-10; 5:7-20 *"we are his workmanship..."*
DAY 4: Philippians 2:12-18 *"...shine as lights in the world..."*
DAY 5: 1 Peter 3:8-17 *"...always being prepared..."*
DAY 6: Luke 4:18 *"He has sent me to proclaim liberty..."*
DAY 7: Colossians 1:9-14 *"...has qualified you to share..."*

OBEY
Head: Think, *"What do I learn about God and people?"*
Heart: Ask, *"God, what are you saying to me today?"*
Hands: Decide, *"How will I respond to God's voice?"*

GOING DEEPER
* What does your unique light look like?
* How can you let this light shine?

15

DENY YOURSELF

> READ LUKE 9:18-36
> "²³ And he said to all, "*If anyone would come after me, let him deny himself and take up his cross daily and follow me.*"

Jesus' challenge to deny ourselves appears to be in complete opposition to our culture. So much of our media, advertising and conversations are about *indulging* ourselves not *denying* ourselves!

In fact, some go further and say that to deny ourselves rather than following our deepest desires is harmful and repressive. However, denying self isn't diminishing self. Rather, it's about following Jesus' example and learning to find meaning and purpose in meeting the needs of others, not just yourself.

This is the point at which the contrast between Jesus and culture is strongest. If only you matter, then denying yourself makes no sense. However, if those around us matter like God says they matter, then there's truly something divine in the idea of denying our own desires and following in Jesus' example.

We know from the record of Jesus' life in the Bible that he didn't *want* to be crucified. Yet, He went through it to fulfil His Father's plan to unite us all together as one family. He believed that his sacrifice would free us from the divisive and destructive power of sin in our lives.

Take time to think of someone who has put your needs above their own. It may have been a mother, father, relative, sibling, friend or mentor. These people are similar to the 'heroes' we mythologise in our greatest books and movies. The ones who saved us from ourselves and the perils around us. While our day-to-day culture encourages indulgence, the timeless stories that we revere across all nations and tribes are almost always about heroes who deny *themselves* for the sake of *others*.

This is why the story of Jesus has transcended 2,000 years of history. He is exactly what our hearts know we need - someone to not just *show* us the way, but to *make* a way for us in the world.

I encourage you to take Jesus' invitation seriously. Embrace his challenge to take up your own opportunities to act with heroic love for the sake of those around you. It's never just about denying or diminishing ourselves. Rather, it's about dedicating our lives for the sake of others, just like he has modelled for us all.

DAILY RHYTHM

PRAY
Centre your mind upon Jesus. Pray, "Come, Holy Spirit".

READ
Make time to read God's Word out loud each day.

DAY 1: Luke 9:23 *"If anyone would come after me..."*

DAY 2: Philippians 2:1-13 *"Jesus, who...emptied himself..."*

DAY 3: Ephesians 4:20-32 *"...put off your old self..."*

DAY 4: Romans 12 *"...your bodies as a living sacrifice, holy..."*

DAY 5: Mark 10:35-45 *"...came not to be served but to serve..."*

DAY 6: Galatians 5:16-26 *"...you will not gratify the desires..."*

DAY 7: Luke 18:18-30 *"Sell all that you have and distribute..."*

OBEY
Head: Think, *"What do I learn about God and people?"*
Heart: Ask, *"God, what are you saying to me today?"*
Hands: Decide, *"How will I respond to God's voice?"*

GOING DEEPER
* What is required for you to move from living for yourself to living for Jesus?

* How can you take up his cross and follow his example?

16

REJOICE AND BE GLAD

> **READ MATTHEW 5:1-12**
> *"[11] "Blessed are you when others revile you and persecute you and utter all kinds of evil against you falsely on my account. [12] Rejoice and be glad, for your reward is great in heaven, for so they persecuted the prophets who were before you."*

Anyone who has tried to follow Jesus knows what it's like to be at least mocked, if not mistreated, for their newfound, Jesus-focused approach to life. Jesus is so sure this is the future for those who follow him that he not only prepares them for it but personally promises to reward all who continue to persevere!

However, in a culture that promotes personal well-being and happiness as the pinnacle experience of life, divine rewards can appear meagre in comparison. Alongside our natural desire for earthly rewards, we also have a never-ending desire for immediate and temporary satisfaction: "I want it now!" However, Jesus wants to open our eyes to the reality that Heaven rewards faithful followers of Jesus with delayed but eternal satisfaction. It is these greater rewards that Jesus says have the power to produce a truer and greater joy within us - even when we are in the midst of persecution for our faith.

Jesus is making it clear that **the rewards we choose to pursue will determine the joy we experience in life.** If we choose to pursue immediate and temporary *earthly* rewards we will receive immediate and temporary joy. If, however, we choose to pursue delayed and eternal *heavenly* rewards we will receive eternal, heavenly joy.

This brings us to the key, transformative point Jesus is making. While heaven's rewards are delayed, Jesus' firm promise that we will receive them is designed to transform our present earthly reality no matter how dire or unjust the circumstances. Even if you were to be mistreated, ridiculed or maligned for following Jesus, you can experience deep internal joy, knowing that deeply satisfying, eternal rewards await you in Heaven.

Have you been excluded for a new approach to finances, relationships or generosity? Be assured you'll be not only rewarded in heaven but surrounded by those who are welcoming you home! Have you been punished by institutions or authorities for pursuing an active living faith? Be assured that in heaven, all those who have suffered like Christ will share in Christ's reward!

So, next time you think or pray, "God, where are you? I'm doing exactly what I think you've asked me to do and I've wound up ridiculed/rejected? What's going on?!" Allow Jesus to remind you that this is not unusual for his followers. Take the opportunity to **exercise your choice to rejoice. Choose to rejoice** in Jesus' promised heavenly rewards rather than complain about the lack of immediate, temporary rewards that can never truly satisfy!

DAILY RHYTHM

PRAY
Centre your mind upon Jesus. Pray, "Come, Holy Spirit".

READ
Make time to read God's Word out loud each day.

DAY 1: Matthew 5:12 *"Rejoice and be glad"*
DAY 2: James 1:1-4, 12 *"...friendship with the world..."*
DAY 3: 2 Corinthians 1:1-10 *"God...comforts us..."*
DAY 4: 2 Corinthians 4:16-18 *"...do not lose heart."*
DAY 5: 1 Peter 1:3-9 *"Do not repay evil for evil..."*
DAY 6: 1 Peter 4:12-19 *"...as you share Christ's sufferings..."*
DAY 7: Philippians 4:1-17 *"Rejoice in the Lord always..."*

OBEY
Head: Think, *"What do I learn about God and people?"*
Heart: Ask, *"God, what are you saying to me today?"*
Hands: Decide, *"How will I respond to God's voice?"*

GOING DEEPER
* What distracts you from God's eternal promises?
* How can you remind yourself of the great hope and eternal promises of God?

17

DO NOT EVEN SIN IN YOUR HEART

> READ MATTHEW 5:27-30
> "But I say to you that **everyone who looks at a woman with lustful intent has already committed adultery with her in his heart.**"

In Matthew chapter 5 from verse 21 through to verse 48 we see Jesus radically altering who we identify as "sinners" and what qualifies as 'sin'.

Jesus' listeners, like many of us, liked to think that sin - murder, anger, adultery, false promises etc - is primarily a problem that *other people* struggle with and will be judged for. Just like His listeners, we use our own categories of sin to declare ourselves "good" and others "sinners". However, Jesus expands our definitions of what sin is and reveals that sin isn't "out there" with *them* but "in here" with *me*.

To illustrate, Jesus says that if you have imagined a sexual fantasy with someone you're not married to, then you are to be judged as equally sinful *as the person who acts out the adulterous fantasy in real life*! In a world of readily available media that facilitates or intentionally promotes sexual fantasy, this may seem quite confronting or even impossible to live out.

Jesus is leading us to conclude that these sins that we desire to enact but restrain ourselves from physically committing (adultery, murder, theft, lying etc) are the sins that reveal not only the *reality* of our hearts but also the *capacity* of our hearts.

See, Jesus' command is not just to remove anything in your life that causes you to sin but to transform the desires of your heart entirely. He knows that if we allow Him access to the very centre of our lives, he can transform our hearts to operate with the full capacity that he originally intended.

Really, Jesus is inviting us to truly "live our best lives". Despite our ability to control any external, observable sin (e.g. adultery, sexual perversion), when we foster sinful sexual desires in our hearts it condemns us to live internally like our worst selves. However, when we learn to foster a life free from sexual perversion in our hearts, our newly found purity encourages us to become like Christ - truly loving those around us without entanglement or ulterior motives. Not only is this Jesus' invitation to us, but this is the life we all know we are designed for and desire to live!

God's heart for his people is not just that they be single and celibate or married and faithful, but pure in heart just like him. As you pursue this renewed heart be mindful that you are working *with* God, not just *for* him. He gives both his Holy Spirit and his truth in the Bible to renew our hearts to be like his. So, I encourage you to take the step of asking him to renew your heart from the inside out.

DAILY RHYTHM

PRAY
Centre your mind upon Jesus. Pray, "Come, Holy Spirit".

READ
Make time to read God's Word out loud each day.

DAY 1: Matthew 5:27-30 *"...adultery...in his heart"*

DAY 2: Hebrews 3 *"...their hearts always turn away from me..."*

DAY 3: Matthew 15:1-20 *"...their hearts are far from me"*

DAY 4: Ephesians 4:17-32 *"...let the Spirit renew your..."*

DAY 5: 1 John 3 *"...we will be like Him..."*

DAY 6: James 4:1-10 *"...God will come close to you"*

DAY 7: Proverbs 4:23 *"Keep your heart with all vigilance..."*

OBEY
Head: Think, *"What do I learn about God and people?"*
Heart: Ask, *"God, what are you saying to me today?"*
Hands: Decide, *"How will I respond to God's voice?"*

GOING DEEPER

* *Describe the heart you think God aspires for us all?*

* *What steps can you take to see God renew your heart from the inside out?*

18

SPEAK SIMPLY + TRUTHFULLY

> READ MATTHEW 5:33-37
> "³⁷ *Let what you say be simply 'Yes' or 'No'; anything more than this comes from evil.*"

When was the last time you stretched the truth, said something you regretted or felt compelled to outline your accomplishments in order to persuade someone to trust you?

These rashly, brashly spoken words can teach us much about the state of our hearts. In vain attempts to be liked, loved and accepted we aim to convince ourselves and others that we are more successful, powerful, knowledgeable, and well-connected than we truly are. Though well-intentioned, Jesus says that our words can betray our sinful desire to always appear "bigger" than we are.

In verses 33-37, Jesus holds up a mirror saying, "Stop aligning yourselves with things bigger than yourselves [heaven, earth, cities] to make out that you are 'somebody to be trusted'." Rather, learn to live and speak with such simplicity and truth that people come to trust you at your word. We shouldn't need to lean on our religion, education, family of origin, successes and fame to convince people we are trustworthy. We should just simply say, "yes" or "no" and leave it at that. Of course, this includes saying, "no", even if it makes us unpopular with those around us!.

Jesus wants the promises we speak to be the promises that we keep. And each time we keep one of our promises or commitments we are actually becoming more like Him. And this is His hope for us, that not only our actions, but our words come to shine bright like His - appealing, inspiring, freeing and encouraging to those around us - without the need for embellishment of any kind.

Jesus is perfectly trustworthy. When he says, "yes", we know he is to be trusted. He has offered us His solemn word that all those who put their faith in Him will be forgiven of their sins, filled with His Spirit and led in a new life of following Him.

Taking Him at his word is called FAITH, and his invitation is to simply say, "Yes"! Not, "Yes, I'll be the best Christian ever". Nor, "I'll never sin again!" But, "Yes, I believe I am who you say I am. You are who you say you are".

This is the greatest, "yes", any of us can speak. If you have not said, "yes", to faith in Jesus, take time to consider if this is what you want. If so, make your own decision to put your faith in Jesus and follow him with your whole life.

You can find some simple guidance on doing this in the *Going 'All In'* section at the beginning of this resource.

DAILY RHYTHM

PRAY
Centre your mind upon Jesus. Pray, "Come, Holy Spirit".

READ
Make time to read God's Word out loud each day.

DAY 1: Matthew 5:33-37 *"...you say be simply 'Yes' or 'No'"*

DAY 2: James 3 *"The tongue is small...but boasts great things"*

DAY 3: Ephesians 4:11-25 *"Speaking the truth in love..."*

DAY 4: 1 John 3:18-24 *"Let us not love in word or talk..."*

DAY 5: 1 Corinthians 2:1-5 *"...my preaching were plain."*

DAY 6: Hebrews 6:13-20 *"God guaranteed it with an oath"*

DAY 7: Proverbs 12:17 *"He who speaks truth tells what..."*

OBEY
> **Head**: Think, *"What do I learn about God and people?"*
> **Heart**: Ask, *"God, what are you saying to me today?"*
> **Hands**: Decide, *"How will I respond to God's voice?"*

GOING DEEPER
* *How can we speak more truthfully and simply?*
* *How can we aim to live in such a way that our lives and words align?*

19

PRACTICE RIGHTEOUSNESS IN SECRET

READ MATTHEW 6:1-4
"*¹ Beware of practicing your righteousness before other people in order to be seen by them,* for then you will have no reward from your Father who is in heaven."

Take a moment to consider, "What's the best piece of advice I've ever received?" "Measure twice, cut once", "Get a haircut, get a real job", "Buy low, sell high", "Be good to your mother"? When Jesus, the most influential person who has ever lived and the Son of God, says, "Beware!", He's warning us that to ignore his advice could be devastating.

In this instance, Jesus is warning us against living out faith in any way that seeks status or reputation as a "spiritual" or "good" person. While there are few of us who ever intend to live this way, it's all too easy to offer an answer, a donation (6:2-4), a prayer (6:5-15) or an invitation primarily because it portrays us in a "good light".

We often behave this way hoping that one day there will be a pay-off of some kind: others will assume we have a superior morality or intellect, we receive invitations to groups or gatherings we've sought access to, or we successfully hide unrighteousness in another hidden part of our life. Jesus says that whenever we play this external reputation game, caring more about who others perceive us to be than who we really are, it's our loss.

As Jesus taught elsewhere, he does willingly reward us for the life we've lived, but he often rewards behaviour that others don't even recognise. In fact, if you read Matthew chapter 6, especially verses 1 to 24, you will see that God is encouraging us to practise our faith secretly, where there's not even the opportunity for our intentions to become warped or reputations to be boosted.

He then says that if we can practise righteousness, prayer, giving and the life of faith *in secret*, we will one day receive a reward that will make a boosted status or elevated reputation seem like a waste of time!

As you reflect upon Matthew 6 and how you are expressing your faith, ask God for a renewed passion for loving Him in secret - praying prayers no one hears and meeting financial needs anonymously. Alongside the joy of unquestioned intentions, we can revel in the knowledge that each small, secret act secures some kind of mysterious, heavenly gift that will make all others pale in comparison!

DAILY RHYTHM

PRAY
Centre your mind upon Jesus. Pray, "Come, Holy Spirit".

READ
Make time to read God's Word out loud each day.

DAY 1: Matthew 6:1-8 *"...your Father who sees in secret..."*

DAY 2: Matthew 23: 1-8 *"...their works they do to be seen..."*

DAY 3: John 13:1-17 *"[as I] have washed your feet, so you..."*

DAY 4: Mark 1:35-39 *"...Jesus got up and went to...pray."*

DAY 5: Luke 18:10-14 *"...those who humble themselves..."*

DAY 6: 1 John 3:16-24 *"we know he lives in us by the Spirit..."*

DAY 7: 1 Peter 5:6 *"Humble yourselves, therefore, under..."*

OBEY
Head: Think, *"What do I learn about God and people?"*
Heart: Ask, *"God, what are you saying to me today?"*
Hands: Decide, *"How will I respond to God's voice?"*

GOING DEEPER
* What "secret" act of righteousness is God calling me to?
* What are the rewards God provides for these secret acts (prayer, giving etc)?

20

LEARN FROM JESUS HOW TO REST

> READ MATTHEW 11:25-30
> "*[28] Come to me, all who labour and are heavy laden, and I will give you rest. [29] Take my yoke upon you, and learn from me, for I am gentle and lowly in heart, and you will find rest for your souls. [30] For my yoke is easy, and my burden is light.*"

If you've ever tried to "measure up" to someone else's expectations for you, then you'll know how tiring it is! This weariness characterised how many people in Jesus' day were experiencing their relationship with God. Jesus pinpointed the root cause of these beliefs in the hypocrisy of the religious leaders of the day. These leaders were falsely teaching that following their rules could lead to favour from God. Rather, these rules led not to God's rest, but wearied and burdened souls.

Even today, if the average person were asked, "What kind of person goes to Heaven?", they are most likely to respond, "A good one". This expectation sounds straightforward, but it usually leads to one of two outcomes, either **hiding** *from* God or **striving** *for* God!

We may hide due to an old addiction that resurfaces, a surprise ending to a relationship or some moment of passion when our resolve to act "good" doesn't match up with the requirements that God, the government or ourselves expect. Amidst failure, "hiders" tend to walk away from church, prayer and sometimes even faith itself.

If you've ever played "hide'n'seek" with a two-year-old, you may have seen them stand in a corner facing the wall with their hands over their eyes, "hiding"! Whenever we try to "hide" from God, the reality is he knows exactly where we are, and what we've done, and is probably having a little chuckle at our efforts. The good news is that Jesus, God's son, came to find "hiders" and heal their hearts.

Others amongst us, full of good intentions, find ourselves striving to meet our expectations of being "good enough". We hope that unlike those around us, we will find a way to "make the cut". If you've ever run this race to be "good enough", you know that as close as you think you get, you never quite "arrive".

Jesus calls us away from both hiding and striving to rest. I imagine this state is like the child above who "hides" in a corner. However, rather than "hiding in plain sight", we are to be "resting in plain sight" - eyes wide open, facing out, ready to be 'found' in our state of perfect rest.

It's to both the striving and the hiding amongst us that Jesus, the Son of God and saviour of the world, gives His invitation. "Come, lay down your burdens and learn from me how to rest. I'm the one you've been looking for. There's no need to hide your sin from me since I've come to heal you. There's no need to earn my favour since I don't reward the morally superior. You can stop aiming to be good for me and allow me to be good towards you. Come and learn from me how to rest."

DAILY RHYTHM

PRAY
Centre your mind upon Jesus. Pray, "Come, Holy Spirit".

READ
Make time to read God's Word out loud each day.

DAY 1: Matthew 11:25-30 *"...to me...and I will give you rest."*

DAY 2: Hebrews 4:8-16 *"...strive to enter that rest."*

DAY 3: Mark 6:6-12 & 30-32 *"...come away...and rest a while"*

DAY 4: 1 John 3:19-24 *"...we know that he abides in us..."*

DAY 5: Psalm 4:8 *"In peace I will both lie down and sleep"*

DAY 6: Psalm 23 *"...I will fear no evil; for you are with me."*

DAY 7: Exodus 33:12-23 *"...and I will give you rest..."*

OBEY
Head: Think, *"What do I learn about God and people?"*
Heart: Ask, *"God, what are you saying to me today?"*
Hands: Decide, *"How will I respond to God's voice?"*

GOING DEEPER
* Are you a "hider" or a "striver"?
* What does it look like for you to rest in Jesus?

21

CLEAN THE INSIDE OF THE CUP

> READ MATTHEW 23:23-28
>
> "²⁵ *"Woe to you, scribes and Pharisees, hypocrites! For you clean the outside of the cup and the plate, but inside they are full of greed and self-indulgence.* ²⁶ *You blind Pharisee!* **First clean the inside of the cup and the plate, so that the outside also may be clean.**"

Have you ever taken a coffee cup out of the dishwasher to make yourself a cuppa only to realise that while it looked clean on the outside, the inside is still full of unremoved grime or detergent? Jesus says that this externally gleaming, but internally grimy cup is representative of a person that spends an inordinate amount of time striving to meet moral or religious expectations, but internally is at least as dark as those over whom they claim moral superiority.

This teaching of Jesus comes right before his execution on

the cross. It's interesting to note that at this culmination of all of his teaching, he is actually asking for what's humanly impossible - to not just purify our behaviour but to perfectly cleanse our hearts. For more of Jesus' teaching on this cleansing, review the first three chapters: *Be Born Again, Repent, Follow Me*.

When our family is on "kitchen duty" there is inevitably one sibling who doesn't meet the "washing up" expectations of another. The repeated reprimand is, "Oi! This bowl isn't clean. Wash it again. If you don't wash all the food off it properly one of us could get sick!" While this rarely leads to an illness, the warning mirrors Jesus' warning. If we are content to scrub the outside of our lives but leave scraps to rot internally, a sickness will manifest within us. Jesus calls this sickness, 'sin'. It's his primary goal to free us from not just the effects of sin, our external behaviour, but the sickness itself, our internal sinful nature.

This is the essence of Jesus' message. Not simply that we are to love those around us, but that we need God's love to invade our hearts. Not simply that we be generous to those in need, but that we invite the truly generous God to dwell within us. Not just that we sacrifice for the good of others, but that we grow a heart like that of Christ who made the ultimate sacrifice for us all. It would be wonderful to see a future in which Jesus' followers are recognised for their good works. However, the ultimate future is one in which followers of Jesus are understood as people with good hearts - restored by God's internal forgiveness of sin, not their external moral striving.

Understanding Jesus' teaching here is critical for not only our own lives but how we relate to those around us! Once we realise that our own, well-intentioned efforts are destined for failure without an internal cleansing, then we can apply the same gracious judgement to those around us. Rather than speaking condemnation upon others for their immoral behaviour, we can share with them that the internal cleansing that Jesus speaks of is available and effective to every one of us. In fact, if they let *him* clean them, they can cease striving to cleanse *themselves*. Have you put your faith in Jesus and his promise to cleanse *you* from the inside out?

DAILY RHYTHM

PRAY
Centre your mind upon Jesus. Pray, "Come, Holy Spirit".

READ
Make time to read God's Word out loud each day.

DAY 1: Matthew 23:1-39 *"...clean the inside of the cup..."*

DAY 2: Matthew 15:1-20 *"...the words you speak come from..."*

DAY 3: Philippians 2:1-18 *"God is working in you..."*

DAY 4: Colossians 2 *"Let your roots grow down into Him..."*

DAY 5: Colossians 3:12-17 *"...let the peace of Christ rule..."*

DAY 6: 1 John 1:5-10 *"God is light, and there is no darkness..."*

DAY 7: Ezekiel 36:26, Hebrews 8:10 *"...you a new heart..."*

OBEY
Head: Think, *"What do I learn about God and people?"*
Heart: Ask, *"God, what are you saying to me today?"*
Hands: Decide, *"How will I respond to God's voice?"*

GOING DEEPER
* *In what ways have you tried to appear clean on the "outside"?*
* *What could it look like to have God cleanse you from the inside out?*

22

TURN THE OTHER CHEEK

READ MATTHEW 5:38-39

"*[38] You have heard that it was said, "An eye for an eye and a tooth for a tooth." [39] But I say to you, Do not resist the one who is evil.* **But if anyone slaps you on the right cheek, turn to him the other also.** *[40] And if anyone would sue you and take your tunic, let him have your cloak as well. [41] And if anyone forces you to go one mile, go with him two miles. [42] Give to the one who begs from you, and do not refuse the one who would borrow from you.*"

When someone tells you to ignore a *minor* injustice done to you by "turning the other cheek", how do you feel? Usually, it doesn't feel great. The advice sounds good to *give*, but is difficult to *receive*. While we easily recognise that it's an upgrade from "an eye for an eye", it often feels like we have to simply "suck it up".

Fortunately, Jesus isn't calling us to *retreat* from revenge into a begrudging pacifism, or even worse, a position of abuse. Rather, he envisions us meeting the needs of "one who begs" or "borrow[s]". This is a call to *advance* his Kingdom over and above our own.

A key contrast between these kingdoms reveals that one is based on protection, while the other is based on provision. While our earthly societies rightly require a foundation of just and godly laws to protect victims and punish perpetrators, Jesus introduces us to a completely uncommon personal foundation based on provision for the needs of those God directs us to help.

When we exercise our personal right to retaliate against someone who has sinned against us, we enter into *their* world - a kingdom dominated by *darkness*. This kingdom prioritises "weighing the scales" to determine what all parties "deserve" and disregards mercy, withholding the punishment others deserve, and grace, giving to others what they do not deserve. In contrast, Jesus' kingdom inverts our impulse for protection and accumulation towards provision and distribution. This otherworldly shift invites those around us into *God's* world - a kingdom of *light*.

Small kindnesses like returning a smile to the person who cuts us off in traffic, or giving a compliment instead of criticism on social media, bring God's light into environments that often look dark. When we begin to provide these small graces, we are not only prepared for the greater ones God calls us to, but we offer a glimpse of a new reality that they desire but are yet to experience.

There is an urgency for us to embrace this life that Jesus marks out for us. Without our willingness to advance his love and light in practical, relational ways, the only guaranteed outcome for the future of the world is continued darkness. So give up your right to protect what you own and take up your responsibility to provide for others as God has provided for you.

DAILY RHYTHM

PRAY
Centre your mind upon Jesus. Pray, "Come, Holy Spirit".

READ
Make time to read God's Word out loud each day.

DAY 1: Matthew 5:38-39 *"...if anyone slaps you on the right..."*
DAY 2: Galatians 6:9 *"Let us not grow weary in doing good..."*
DAY 3: 1 Peter 2:23 *"He did not retaliate when he was..."*
DAY 4: Proverbs 15:1 *"A gentle answer deflects anger..."*
DAY 5: Luke 23:34 *"Father forgive them for they don't know..."*
DAY 6: John 10:18 *"No one can take my life from me..."*
DAY 7: Romans 12:9-21 *"Repay no one evil for evil..."*

OBEY
Head: Think, *"What do I learn about God and people?"*
Heart: Ask, *"God, what are you saying to me today?"*
Hands: Decide, *"How will I respond to God's voice?"*

GOING DEEPER
* *In what ways has my desire for justice been a desire for retaliation?*
* *In what areas of life can I exercise active, healthy love out of obedience to Jesus?*

23

BE PERFECT, AS YOUR FATHER IS PERFECT

READ MATTHEW 5:43-48

[43] "You have heard that it was said, 'You shall love your neighbor and hate your enemy.' [44] But I say to you, Love your enemies and pray for those who persecute you, [45] so that you may be sons of your Father who is in heaven. For he makes his sun rise on the evil and on the good, and sends rain on the just and on the unjust. [46] For if you love those who love you, what reward do you have? Do not even the tax collectors do the same? [47] And if you greet only your brothers, what more are you doing than others? Do not even the Gentiles do the same? [48] You therefore must be perfect, as your heavenly Father is perfect."

When Jesus calls us to be "perfect" it can feel like an impossible dream. How could someone who knows "everything" not see what is clear to all of us - no one has ever come close to being "perfect"?

However, the key point is not that God is calling us to a new rules-based religion but to a new family. Jesus calling us sons reminds us that we are God's much-loved children adopted into His family. Metaphorically, we are carrying our heavenly father's DNA.

If you've ever watched a child pretend to "cook" pizza on a plastic stove or "mowing" the lawn with a tiny, plastic mower, you'll notice their attempts to be like their parents are clumsy and comical. Yet we encourage them rather than mock them. Why? Because each of these activities gives the child a chance to live out their design and desire to grow up to be like their parent(s).

This is the life I believe Jesus is calling each of us to. He's reminding us how our heavenly dad loves others - without discrimination or limit - and that as His children it is our God-given design and desire to learn to live and love just like Him.

The word "perfect" here is not used to mean moral flawlessness but spiritual maturity. In other words, it's an invitation and encouragement to grow up to live and love just like your heavenly dad.

So remember, your dad designed you to be like Him. While your feeble attempts to live like your dad may look comical to everyone watching, God smiles as he watches you. He believes you can fulfil your God-given design to live and love as he does.

So, cast aside every doubt and all shame and learn to love as our heavenly dad does.

DAILY RHYTHM

PRAY
Centre your mind upon Jesus. Pray, "Come, Holy Spirit".

READ
Make time to read God's Word out loud each day.

DAY 1: Matthew 5:43-48 *"...be perfect..."*
DAY 2: Matthew 18:21-35 *"How often will...I forgive..."*
DAY 3: Luke 15:11-32 *"...my son was dead, and is alive..."*
DAY 4: 1 Cor 13:1-13 *"...faith, hope and love..."*
DAY 5: Romans 12:9-21 *"Love each other with genuine..."*
DAY 6: 1 John 4:7-21 *"...all who live in love live in God"*
DAY 7: Psalm 145 *"The LORD is gracious and merciful..."*

OBEY
Head: Think, "What do I learn about God and people?"
Heart: Ask, "God, what are you saying to me today?"
Hands: Decide, "How will I respond to God's voice?"

GOING DEEPER
* What does it mean for you to know that you are part of God's family?
* In what ways do you need to learn to love like your heavenly dad?

24

WATCH + PRAY TO AVOID TEMPTATION

> MATTHEW 26:36-45
> "⁴⁰ And he came to the disciples and found them sleeping. And he said to Peter, "So, could you not watch with me one hour? ⁴¹ **Watch and pray that you may not enter into temptation. The spirit indeed is willing, but the flesh is weak.**"

It's easy to cruise through life parroting the iconic phrase from the first LEGO movie, "Everything is awesome". Sometimes, everything *is* awesome. That is, of course, until it isn't.

Unlike some of our idealistic views of reality, Jesus knows that eventually all of us will be "caught out" by temptation. Like us, three of Jesus' closest companions, Peter, James and John, got completely caught out the night their leader was arrested in the garden of Gethsemane.

While Jesus prayed for the strength to submit to his unjust arrest and death, they slept. While Jesus knew what was coming, his followers didn't. Despite having told them trials were coming, they may have thought, "Everything is awesome. Jesus is on our side and he is winning. We're unstoppable!" Yet Jesus knew that literally overnight one of His most ardent supporters, Peter, would - in moments of *fleshly* self-preservation - deny that he even knew who Jesus was!

Like Peter, James and John, we need to be alert to the reality that our strength of spirit and bold intentions ("everything is awesome"!) can be exactly what blinds us to just how weak our flesh is.

If we can grasp this reality, we can see that Jesus wasn't just preparing Himself for the path ahead, but modelling the way for those who would follow Him. He both "called out" their weaknesses and simultaneously modelled the solution - passionate, *pre-emptive* prayer.

When the disciples asked Jesus how to pray in chapter 6 of Matthew ("teach us to pray Lord"), they likely wanted to know the secrets of praying like Jesus. They wanted access to the privilege of talking with God in the intimate and powerful way Jesus did. It would have appeared to be a new level of spiritual life - one they all wanted access to.

However, it seems that in the garden on that fateful night, Jesus revealed to them that it's not just a spiritual privilege to pray, it's a personal, physical *necessity*. When your spirit is willing but your flesh is weak, Jesus says you need to pray. This prayer is not just to avoid temptation, but to overcome the flesh in order to continue to follow Jesus wherever he leads.

Like Jesus and his disciples, what's at stake is our purpose. To complete his purpose on earth, Jesus needed to pray. To overcome the temptation to give up on *your* purpose, *you* need to pray in order to overcome the weakness of your flesh and live the full life Jesus has called you to!

DAILY RHYTHM

PRAY
Centre your mind upon Jesus. Pray, "Come, Holy Spirit".

READ
Make time to read God's Word out loud each day.

DAY 1: Matthew 26:31-46, 69-75 *"Watch and pray..."*

DAY 2: Matthew 6:5-13 *"Our Father in heaven..."*

DAY 3: Romans 7:14-8:4 *"Who will free me from this life...?"*

DAY 4: Romans 8:5-17 *"...the Spirit gives you life..."*

DAY 5: Romans 8:18-30 *"...the Holy Spirit helps us..."*

DAY 6: Galatians 5:1-26 *"So Christ has truly set us free."*

DAY 7: Romans 8:28 *"...in all things God works for the good..."*

OBEY
Head: Think, *"What do I learn about God and people?"*
Heart: Ask, *"God, what are you saying to me today?"*
Hands: Decide, *"How will I respond to God's voice?"*

GOING DEEPER
* *Where in your life is your spirit willing but your flesh weak?*
* *How might prayer help you overcome your flesh and temptation?*

25

BE ON YOUR GUARD AGAINST ALL COVETOUSNESS

READ LUKE 12:13-21

[13] *Someone in the crowd said to him, "Teacher, tell my brother to divide the inheritance with me."* [14] *But he said to him, "Man, who made me a judge or arbitrator over you?"* [15] ***And he said to them, "Take care, and be on your guard against all covetousness, for one's life does not consist in the abundance of his possessions."*** [16] *And he told them a parable, saying, "The land of a rich man produced plentifully,* [17] *and he thought to himself, 'What shall I do, for I have nowhere to store my crops?'* [18] *And he said, 'I will do this: I will tear down my barns and build larger ones, and there I will store all my grain and my goods.* [19] *And I will say to my soul, "Soul, you have ample goods laid up for many years; relax, eat, drink, be merry."'*

> [20] *But God said to him, 'Fool! This night your soul is required of you, and the things you have prepared, whose will they be?'* [21] *So is the one who lays up treasure for himself and is not rich toward God."*

Jesus spoke a lot about treasure. This wasn't because *he* was obsessed with silver and gold, but because *we* are. Knowing that material riches are capable of robbing us of true riches, he reminds us that our hearts both reveal and determine what we truly treasure. It's not that all rich people are covetous (envious of others' things), but that *all* our hearts are susceptible to the pursuit of temporary rather than eternal riches.

The "rich fool" (as he's come to be known in Christian culture) in Jesus' story sought to silence the deepest, healthy desires of his soul by telling it to, "relax, eat, drink, be merry". We may not all be wealthy, but many of us can relate to masking the deep, God-given desires of our hearts with all manner of temporary luxuries. While for centuries people binged on food, drink and sex, we're taking it to new levels. We have unimaginable access to endless menus, shows, pornography and sports to escape our deepest needs. If we aren't secure in our own home and lifestyle we're able to visit the far-flung corners of the earth at relatively low cost! Rather than opening our lives to those who live around us, we can now 'connect' online with endless strangers we'll never meet.

Much of this stems from a covetous spirit. We perceive what others have - a perfect, dramatic or adventurous life; sexual fulfilment; earthly fame; global adventures; large followings or popularity - and we hope that our own possession of such things will fill the gap in our own souls. We tell our souls, "Put aside your God-given inclinations and be satisfied with this popular, short-term solution I've found". We tell ourselves, "You just need a little *more* 'me-time' this week."

To these hungry souls Jesus says, "Beware!" Covetousness is not just a sign of deep and damaging insecurity, but it leads to a wasted life. In allowing our souls' inbuilt desire for God and his goodness to be replaced with covetousness, we miss out on the deepest treasures God has in store for us. Rather, Jesus encourages us to "be rich toward God". Much could be said about what this entails, but maybe the simplest explanation is to allow your soul to feast on God, his goodness, his word (the Bible), his Holy Spirit and the life his son Jesus offers to all through faith.

DAILY RHYTHM

PRAY
Centre your mind upon Jesus. Pray, "Come, Holy Spirit".

READ
Make time to read God's Word out loud each day.

DAY 1: Luke 12:13-21 *"...guard against all covetousness..."*
DAY 2: Matthew 13:45-47 *"...kingdom of heaven is like a..."*
DAY 3: Philippians 4:10-13 *"...situation I am to be content."*
DAY 4: Galatians 6:6-9 *"...for whatever one sows, that will..."*
DAY 5: Luke 6:27-36 *"Give to everyone who begs from you..."*
DAY 6: James 3:13-8, 4:13-17 *"...What is your life?"*
DAY 7: Galatians 5:16-26 *"...the flesh are against the Spirit..."*

OBEY
Head: Think, *"What do I learn about God and people?"*
Heart: Ask, *"God, what are you saying to me today?"*
Hands: Decide, *"How will I respond to God's voice?"*

GOING DEEPER
* What items, experiences or people do we want to possess in our culture?
* What could it look like for you to be "rich toward God"?

PART 3

OTHERS

26

LOVE YOUR NEIGHBOUR AS YOURSELF

> READ MATT 22:34-40
> "³⁷ And he said to him, "**You shall love the Lord your God with all your heart and with all your soul and with all your mind.** ³⁸ **This is the great and first commandment.** ³⁹ **And a second is like it: You shall love your neighbour as yourself.** ⁴⁰ On these two commandments depend all the Law and the Prophets."

In discussing modern morality, Christians often spruik that we should, "Love the sinner but hate the sin". Christian theologian C.S. Lewis initially considered this saying quite silly until he realised that he had inadvertently been loving one sinner in this manner his whole life - himself. He says:

"You are told to love your neighbour as yourself. How do you love yourself? When I look into my own mind, I find that I do not love myself by thinking myself a dear old chap or having *affectionate feelings. I do not think that I love myself because I am particularly good, but just because I am myself and quite apart from my character. I might detest something which I have done. Nevertheless, I do not cease to love myself. In other words, that definite distinction that Christians make between hating sin and loving the sinner is one that you have been making in your own case since you were born. You dislike what you have done, but you don't cease to love yourself. You may even think that you ought to be hanged. You may even think that you ought to go to the Police and own up and be hanged. Love is not affectionate feeling, but a steady wish for the loved person's ultimate good as far as it can be obtained."* - C.S. Lewis, *The Problem of Pain*, 1940

This powerful realisation offers us an incredible internal challenge. If we are so adept at love, why are we so willing to offer it to ourselves but so challenged to offer it beyond ourselves? As C.S. Lewis discovered, self-love is natural to all of us. This is why Jesus so confidently bases his command on two universal facts. Fact one, we have a seemingly unlimited capacity for self-love. Fact two, we do not love our "neighbour" as Jesus modelled, or even as we desire ourselves!

Given our lack of 'natural' capacity, we require not just a "better" love, but a new nature. This internal 'gap' between our original nature and our preferred one is the gap that Jesus came to not only reveal but to recover. His sacrificial death in our place removes not just the guilt of our sin, but gives us a new, "resurrected" life just like his. This new nature has a capacity for love that our old nature didn't. This is an ancient idea that God introduces in Genesis. He says we are all created in His image and designed to live accordingly. Jesus' invitation to follow him in a life of love literally returns us to the kind of life we were originally designed to live!

So, do you graciously "see the best" in yourself despite your sin? If so, how might you learn from Jesus how to love others in the same way you have loved yourself?

DAILY RHYTHM

PRAY
Centre your mind upon Jesus. Pray, "Come, Holy Spirit".

READ
Make time to read God's Word out loud each day.

DAY 1: Matt 22:37-40 "...You shall love your neighbour.."
DAY 2: Luke 3:10-12 "...If you have two shirts, give one to..."
DAY 3: James 2:1-13, 14-26 "...never think some people..."
DAY 4: 1 Tim 1:1-17 "...Jesus came into the world to save..."
DAY 5: Matthew 18:21–35 "...as I had mercy on you?"
DAY 6: Ephesians 4:31-2 "Be kind, ...forgiving one another..."
DAY 7: Phil 2:1-11 "...look not only to his own interests..."

OBEY
Head: Think, *"What do I learn about God and people?"*
Heart: Ask, *"God, what are you saying to me today?"*
Hands: Decide, *"How will I respond to God's voice?"*

GOING DEEPER
* How do you desire to be treated on your worst day?
* What needs to change in your life for you to live like this towards those around you?

27

INVITE THE UNINVITED INTO YOUR LIFE

READ LUKE 14:12-24

*"¹² He said also to the man who had invited him, "When you give a dinner or a banquet, do not invite your friends or your brothers or your relatives or rich neighbours, lest they also invite you in return and you be repaid. ¹³ **But when you give a feast, invite the poor, the crippled, the lame, the blind, ¹⁴ and you will be blessed, because they cannot repay you. For you will be repaid at the resurrection of the just.""***

There's something satisfying about knowing that Jesus loved to party and even gave instructions for his followers for when (not *if*!) we "feast" [party]. However, Jesus clarifies that the way we party and who we party with reveals the intentions of our hearts. When we consider who we invite to the beach, a BBQ, movie night or dinner party we often see that much of what we do in life, even our hospitality and celebrations, are done for "kickbacks".

In this encounter, Jesus calls us to rethink how we party and who we party with. He's calling for us to not just change up the guest list but to re-organise how we host people in our lives so that it's almost impossible to receive any earthly reward whatsoever. This new approach to hospitality disregards the praise of the elite in favour of heavenly rewards that no earthly currency or reputation can compare.

If you've ever shared a meal in a home with a newly arrived refugee you'll know the powerful psychological, emotional and physical impact an invitation can have upon an individual or family. Long-term Australians share birthdays, and BBQs and often "grab a cuppa" without giving it too much thought. However, new Australians are rarely invited into these gatherings that we largely take for granted! At least part of their absence at our gatherings could be a culture gap. They may not provide the fancy food, gossip or social media clout we selfishly use to boost our own reputation or sense of worth.

The "feasts" that Jesus encourages us to host are the ones that explicitly include those who have nothing to offer us! Furthermore, when we are willing to welcome those whom he welcomes, he guarantees both an *earthly blessing* and a *heavenly reward*!

What would it look like for you to let Jesus re-organise your calendar and plan your guest list?

DAILY RHYTHM

PRAY
Centre your mind upon Jesus. Pray, "Come, Holy Spirit".

READ
Make time to read God's Word out loud each day.

DAY 1: Luke 14:1-24 *"...when you give a feast, invite the poor..."*

DAY 2: 1 Corinthians 1:26-31 *"...the world considers foolish..."*

DAY 3: James 2:1-13 *"But if you show partiality..."*

DAY 4: Matthew 25:31-46 *"I was hungry and you gave..."*

DAY 5: Mark 12:28-34 *"...Which commandment is the..."*

DAY 6: Romans 12:9-21 *"...seek to show hospitality."*

DAY 7: Psalm 68:6 NLT *"God places the lonely in families;"*

OBEY
Head: Think, *"What do I learn about God and people?"*
Heart: Ask, *"God, what are you saying to me today?"*
Hands: Decide, *"How will I respond to God's voice?"*

GOING DEEPER
* Have you been shown meaningful hospitality?
* How could you re-organise your time to include someone who is often excluded?

28

BE RECONCILED

> **READ MATTHEW 5:23-24**
> *"So if you are offering your gift at the altar and there remember that your brother has something against you, leave your gift there before the altar and go. **First be reconciled to your brother, and then come and offer your gift.**"*

In Jesus' day, religious people would sacrifice to God as both an act of worship and a means of forgiveness for their sins so that they might again be reconciled to God. Amongst this familiar practice, Jesus was about to offer himself as a *once-forever* divine sacrifice to provide *permanent* forgiveness of sins. In replacing this sacrificial system, Jesus provides a poignant reminder that the reconciliation he offers us is not a token religious act, but a relational one. Unlike merely transactional forgiveness, Jesus highlights that the damage sin does is not just between us and God but also between ourselves and those around us.

Jesus spotlights the need for reconciliation by using the

word 'brother' to show that if you are a person of faith, then those who share your faith are in effect part of God's family with you. As siblings in God's family, it's incongruous with God's "family values" that one of his children can be at peace with him, but at war with a sibling. How could someone who claims to be reconciled with God not be willing to reconcile with other men and women whom God has also reconciled to himself and brought into His family?

We know how serious a point Jesus is making because we presume from the details of the story that he is teaching this in Galilee, which was approximately 80 miles from the temple in Jerusalem - the only place where a Jewish altar for animal sacrifice existed at the time. So Jesus is declaring that God sees personal reconciliation as such a significant spiritual act that if you arrived in Jerusalem to worship God but realised that someone has a valid complaint against you back home, then you must quickly double back to *set things right*. Given that Jesus was speaking to people in Galilee at the time, about four days walk from Jerusalem, walking home to reconcile with a "brother" before returning to worship would have sounded quite extreme to his audience! Yet Jesus is clearly teaching that unless they had made a sincere attempt to reconcile with people in their life, they shouldn't seek reconciliation with God through their temple worship.

Since Jesus' death has made it clear that his personal sacrifice was the last sacrifice that would ever be needed, we no longer need to make sacrifices at any altar or payments to any account to be forgiven. However, whenever we pray or worship the God who has reconciled us to himself, Jesus would have us consider if there is anyone else with whom we have not yet reconciled. If there is, then Jesus would advise us to "go" and hear them out, display compassion and understanding and ultimately apologise and forgive wherever necessary. This is how we live out the reconciliation we have received in Jesus. Is there someone in God's family that you need to reconcile with?

DAILY RHYTHM

PRAY
Centre your mind upon Jesus. Pray, "Come, Holy Spirit".

READ
Make time to read God's Word out loud each day.

DAY 1: Matthew 5:23-24 *"...be reconciled to your brother..."*

DAY 2: Colossians 3:1-17 *"...if one has a complaint against..."*

DAY 3: Matthew 6:9-15 *"...forgive us our debts, as we also..."*

DAY 4: James 5:13-16 *"...confess your sins to one another..."*

DAY 5: 1 Cor 5:18-20 *"...reconciled us to himself and gave..."*

DAY 6: Hebrews 12:12-17 *"Strive for peace with everyone..."*

DAY 7: Proverbs 25:21-22 *"...burning coals on his head..."*

OBEY
Head: Think, *"What do I learn about God and people?"*
Heart: Ask, *"God, what are you saying to me today?"*
Hands: Decide, *"How will I respond to God's voice?"*

GOING DEEPER
* What damage has unresolved conflict done to you?
* What could be possible if you were to courageously risk reconciling a past relationship?

29

LOVE YOUR ENEMIES

READ LUKE 6:27-36
³⁵ But love your enemies, and do good, and lend, expecting nothing in return, and your reward will be great, and you will be sons of the Most High, for he is kind to the ungrateful and the evil. ³⁶ Be merciful, even as your Father is merciful."

When people are asked about their guiding principle in life, it's not uncommon to hear them say something like, "Love everybody". Even modern-day companies like Google have built momentum around their early motto, "Don't be evil." However, while these statements contain a sense of virtue, they actually fall incredibly short of Jesus' disruptive call to "love your *enemies*".

When we say we want to 'love everybody', we are usually expressing our intentions, feelings or aspirations to simply have good vibes towards everyone we happen to meet day-to-day. While this is certainly to be encouraged, it doesn't require any of us to love in such a way that we are actively, sacrificially bringing kindness into the lives of those around us. And while living by the principle of "don't be evil" sounds noble, it would certainly be possible to retain deep resentment towards another and still meet the requirements of "don't be evil".

To corporations and individuals alike, Jesus offers a far nobler and divine invitation. He says we are to love - bless, pray and lend to - even those who hold evil intentions towards us. Simply possessing loving feelings or sympathy towards those whose hearts are filled with hatred doesn't cut it. Rather, we are to live with a proactive, hands-on kind of love.

This kind of unnatural love can only be attained by the love within you being greater than the evil around you. This is why Christ's command seems at odds with our natural understanding and experience of reality. Without possessing Christ's love within us, it's an entirely unreasonable request. However, if by faith we can obtain his love in our hearts, it then becomes possible to embody this other-worldly love for those who have wronged us in our everyday lives. In this way, we approach Christ's goal for us of becoming "merciful, even as your Father is merciful."

When this internal-external alignment does not happen, we become hypocrites, failing to live as we know we ought. We might know God's love in our hearts but fail to act accordingly.

Alternatively, we might aim to love like Christ but perform out of duty, rather than true love. This too is a misaligned, hypocritical life.

Jesus, however, is the perfect embodiment of this lovingly aligned life. Though at some point we have all been his 'enemy', His love didn't just dwell *within* him. Rather his love flowed *out* onto the cross to set us free from sin and self! Truly, he has embraced us even while we were still sinners, enemies of the truth that emanates from him. What would it take for us to love our enemies as he has loved us?

DAILY RHYTHM

PRAY
Centre your mind upon Jesus. Pray, "Come, Holy Spirit".

READ
Make time to read God's Word out loud each day.

DAY 1: Luke 6:27-36 *"But love your enemies, and do good..."*
DAY 2: Acts 9:1-19 *"I am Jesus, whom you are persecuting."*
DAY 3: Matthew 8:5-13 *"Lord, my servant is lying..."*
DAY 4: Luke 10:25:37 *"And who is my neighbour?"*
DAY 5: Acts 7:54-60 *"Lord, do not hold this sin against them."*
DAY 6: Luke 23:23-43 *"Truly, I say to you, today you will..."*
DAY 7: 1 Samuel 24:1-22 *"...I will not put out my hand..."*

OBEY
Head: Think, *"What do I learn about God and people?"*
Heart: Ask, *"God, what are you saying to me today?"*
Hands: Decide, *"How will I respond to God's voice?"*

GOING DEEPER
* Does anyone in your life consider you an "enemy"?
* What would be the first step to loving this person like Jesus?

30

JUDGE NOT, THAT YOU BE NOT JUDGED

> READ MATTHEW 7:1-5
>
> ***"Judge not, that you be not judged. For with the judgement you pronounce you will be judged, and with the measure you use it will be measured to you.*** *Why do you see the speck that is in your brother's eye, but do not notice the log that is in your own eye? Or how can you say to your brother, 'Let me take the speck out of your eye,' when there is the log in your own eye? You hypocrite, first take the log out of your own eye, and then you will see clearly to take the speck out of your brother's eye."*

Has anyone ever said to you after you gave them some advice or correction, "Stop judging me?" After all, doesn't Jesus say, "Don't judge"? Well, yes, but he offers more than that. He gives three reasons to rethink our instincts to "judge" others.

Firstly if judgement on sin is what we seek - *for others* - then he says judgement on sin is what we'll get - *for ourselves*. This form of "natural justice" simply seeks to identify and punish sin wherever we find it. The inverse of Jesus' 'golden rule' (Luke 6:31) is essentially, "Judge others as you would have them judge you." *Secondly*, Jesus reminds us that God's unique perspective on sin means he is privy to see it within us *all*. His stark reminder is that God can see more sin in us than we can ever find in someone else. *Thirdly*, the use of the word "brother" gives us a gentle reminder that we all share the same human predisposition to sin as the men and women we judge. We also share the same loving creator, and, in the case of those who also follow Jesus, have been gifted to us as an eternal family.

So, when we sense the urge to judge someone, Jesus encourages us to pause and reconsider how transparently he sees our interactions with others. He will judge as we judge others. He sees our own sin like no one else does. He invites us to value others as members of his family, not inferiors.

Jesus concludes that he will teach those who grapple with their own sin how to *"see clearly to take the speck out of your brother's eye"*. This doesn't mean we take the role of judge in everyone's lives, but that we humbly offer our experience of identifying and removing sins in our life to others. Rather than being a weapon of judgement upon others, this skill becomes a gift of grace and healing to those around us who seek our help.

Notably, Jesus identifies the sin in question as merely a "speck", which is likely a subtle nudge from Jesus to question if the sin that originally upset us so much is even worth mentioning at all. In light of Jesus, much of what bothers us can simply be overlooked.

Why not take a moment to reflect upon the following question, *"How do I want to be judged?"*

DAILY RHYTHM

PRAY
Centre your mind upon Jesus. Pray, "Come, Holy Spirit".

READ
Make time to read God's Word out loud each day.

DAY 1: Matthew 7:1-2 *"Judge not, that you be not judged."*

DAY 2: Galatians 6:1-10 *"Bear one another's burdens..."*

DAY 3: James 4:1-12 *"God opposes the proud but gives grace..."*

DAY 4: Romans 14:1-13 *"For we will all stand before..."*

DAY 5: 1 Corinthians 4:1-5 *"...who will bring to light.."*

DAY 6: John 8:1-11 *"Let him who is without sin among you..."*

DAY 7: James 1:19-27 *"...be quick to hear, slow to speak..."*

OBEY
Head: Think, *"What do I learn about God and people?"*
Heart: Ask, *"God, what are you saying to me today?"*
Hands: Decide, *"How will I respond to God's voice?"*

GOING DEEPER

* Describe a time when you've been "judged" unfairly.

* Given your current thoughts and life, how would you like to be judged by God and others?

31

DON'T REPLACE GOD'S COMMANDS WITH YOUR TRADITIONS

READ MATTHEW 15:1-20

"*³ Jesus replied, "And why do you, by your traditions, violate the direct commandments of God?* ⁴ *For instance, God says, 'Honour your father and mother,' and 'Anyone who speaks disrespectfully of father or mother must be put to death.'* ⁵ *But you say it is all right for people to say to their parents, 'Sorry, I can't help you. For I have vowed to give to God what I would have given to you.'* ⁶ *In this way, you say they don't need to honour their parents. And so you cancel the word of God for the sake of your own tradition."* (NLT)

Human beings have a strong tendency to assert themselves above God. One of our sneakiest and most harmful strategies is to add our own take on God's commands. This disregards the purity of God's commands, adds contrived burdens to the lives of those around us and, cruelly, promises them that if they meet the demands, God will reward them. Jesus notes that the religious leaders of the day have taken this to an extreme, by creating [religious] traditions that actually encourage people to "violate the direct commandments of God". He uses one example of this to drive home not only the violation at play but also the importance of the original command to, "Honour your father and mother".

As a religious Jew, Jesus and his community were bound by God's command to 'honour your father and mother', which included financial provision in their old age. However, a religious practice called *corban* evolved to provide a financial loophole for people who wanted to appear religious but keep their wealth to themselves. *Corban* allowed voluntary pledges of money or materials to the temple. While technically "given" to the temple treasury, donors were still able to access those funds provided they were used exclusively for *their own personal needs*. Rather than "honouring" their parents as God had commanded, adult children could declare to their parents, "I'd love to meet *your* financial needs, but I've pledged all my savings to God and I couldn't possibly break my promise to him!" *Corban* enabled people to be honoured in the community as "generous" while living in direct rebellion to God. This enabled greed to masquerade as generosity.

Jesus' warning should cause us to consider our own life.

Do we practice any accepted religious or cultural traditions that fly in the face of God's commands? It could be going into debt to fund a church project instead of meeting the needs of family, friends or neighbours. It could be a full week of church activities instead of sharing even one meal with a spouse, parent, sibling, child or relative who is isolated. It could be endless availability to mentor or pray with other Christians, but a lack of interest in those God holds us responsible for. While participating in traditions that give us a reputation or applause is tempting, it can easily masquerade as an unwillingness to obey God's commands.

So, are there any "Christian" practices that have limited you from honouring the family God has placed you in? Have your family's imperfections given you an excuse for not honouring them?

DAILY RHYTHM

PRAY
Centre your mind upon Jesus. Pray, "Come, Holy Spirit".

READ
Make time to read God's Word out loud each day.

DAY 1: Matthew 15:1-9 *"Honour your father and your..."*

DAY 2: Exodus 20:1-19, Deuteronomy 5:16 *"...that your..."*

DAY 3: Ephesians 6:1-4 *"Honour your father and mother..."*

DAY 4: 1 Timothy 5:1-8 *"Do not rebuke an older man..."*

DAY 5: 2 Timothy 3:1-5 *"In the last days...people will be..."*

DAY 6: Romans 13:1-13 *"Let every person be subject to the..."*

DAY 7: Proverbs 1:8, 23:22 *"...do not despise your mother..."*

OBEY
Head: Think, *"What do I learn about God and people?"*
Heart: Ask, *"God, what are you saying to me today?"*
Hands: Decide, *"How will I respond to God's voice?"*

GOING DEEPER
* Were your parents/guardians honoured or dishonoured?
* Why do you think God is so strong about the need for children to honour their parents?

32

HUMBLE YOURSELF LIKE A CHILD

READ MATTHEW 18:1-4
"At that time the disciples came to Jesus, saying, "Who is the greatest in the kingdom of heaven?" And calling to him a child, he put him in the midst of them and said, "Truly, I say to you, unless you change and become like children, you will never enter the kingdom of heaven. **Whoever humbles himself like this child is the greatest in the kingdom of heaven."**

While our culture often idolises the vigour of youth, most kids "can't wait to grow up"! Despite missing the innocence and freedom of a normal childhood, most adults are glad to have left behind their child-ish *Peter Pan*-like thoughts and behaviours!

We know from the additional details in the gospel of Mark (see Mark 10:15) that the disciples held similar beliefs. To them, childhood and children were a necessary inconvenience. However, Jesus counters his apprentices with two points that are fundamentally at odds with their natural mindset: (1) God deeply values children and childhood, and (2) the humility of a child's state in life reflects the humility required for anyone to come into a relationship with God.

One of the most beautiful and vulnerable aspects of a child's life is their reliance upon benevolent "grown-ups". On their journey to understanding self, others and the world children require sustenance, shelter and oversight. In this way, no child is truly "self-made". Their very survival and success in the world are entirely reliant upon others.

Similarly, Jesus says it's impossible to enter into God's Kingdom on our own efforts. None of us are "self-made". We rely on God's love to seek us out, Jesus' sacrifice to redeem us and His power to restore us to a new path.

So while many leaders, gurus and coaches implore us to "step up", Jesus calls us to "step down" into child-like dependence upon Him. This is why Jesus insisted that we didn't need just a new *direction* in life, but a completely new start in life. This new life requires the humility to learn new desires, hopes, beliefs and loves. This is what is required to live in the kingdom Jesus invites us to. To turn back the clock and be reborn by God into a completely new, humble, child-like faith.

DAN HARDING

What needs to change for you to become like a child, humbly trusting Jesus for all your needs?

DAILY RHYTHM

PRAY
Centre your mind upon Jesus. Pray, "Come, Holy Spirit".

READ
Make time to read God's Word out loud each day.

DAY 1: Matthew 18:1-14 *"Whoever humbles himself like..."*
DAY 2: Mark 10:13-16 *"Let the children come to me;..."*
DAY 3: Deuteronomy 6:1-9 *"You shall teach them..."*
DAY 4: Luke 9:44-48 *"Whoever receives this child in my..."*
DAY 5: Psalm 127 *"Behold, children are a heritage from..."*
DAY 6: Ephesians 6:1-4 *"Fathers, do not provoke your..."*
DAY 7: Luke 22:24-30 *"...among you as the one who serves."*

OBEY
Head: Think, *"What do I learn about God and people?"*
Heart: Ask, *"God, what are you saying to me today?"*
Hands: Decide, *"How will I respond to God's voice?"*

GOING DEEPER
* How do you personally view children and childhood?
* How could your attitudes towards children more closely align with those of Jesus?

33

FORGIVE THOSE WHO SIN AGAINST YOU

> **READ MATTHEW 18:21-35**
> *"²¹ Then Peter came up and said to him, "Lord, how often will my brother sin against me, and I forgive him? As many as seven times?" ²² Jesus said to him, "I do not say to you seven times, but seventy-seven times."*

The decision to forgive can be costly. To cancel the debt you're owed and to let go of anger or resentment towards another requires personal sacrifice. Despite the cost, many of us are happy to pay the price and feel satisfied that we've taken the higher, moral ground. However, when we encounter a "serial offender", our goodwill runs dry and we resent being expected or asked to forgive.

When our resolve dissipates, Jesus' call to forgive "seventy-seven times" might feel unfair or even harmful. We may justify withholding forgiveness by saying, "They need to learn a lesson!" Or "I'm not a doormat!" No matter how justified we feel in saying this, in essence, we are deciding that our decision to *not* forgive someone not only benefits them (!) but is somehow the right moral decision for us.

It's at this point that we need to ask ourselves, "Has someone *not* forgiving *me* ever helped me overcome my sin?" The answer is obvious. Forgiveness provides the most transformative outcome in the life of the sinner. While it doesn't guarantee future behaviour, true forgiveness introduces the concept of *mercy*, not receiving what we deserve. Mercy prepares us to meet *grace*, being given what we don't deserve. And it is grace that provides the environment and the fuel for internal *transformation*.

Forgiveness is thus not just about moral virtue, but about inviting those who have offended us into a whole new way of thinking, living and relating. A life marked by mercy, not malice. A life marked by grace, not guilt.

Our ability to consistently offer this costly forgiveness to others correlates strongly with our own experience of forgiveness. It may be our parents, spouse or friend who enriched our hearts with grace. Or maybe it was and is Jesus. His sacrificial forgiveness of us is not conditioned upon our ability to immediately obey him in every way. Rather, his merciful offering of grace to us is the fuel for our merciful offerings of grace to others - even seventy-seven times.

Who has graciously forgiven you? Who do you need to pray
for help to graciously forgive?

DAILY RHYTHM

PRAY
Centre your mind upon Jesus. Pray, "Come, Holy Spirit".

READ
Make time to read God's Word out loud each day.

DAY 1: Matt 18:21-35 *"...sin against me, and I forgive him?"*

DAY 2: Luke 17:1-10 *"If your brother...repents, forgive him,"*

DAY 3: Colossians 3:12-17 *"...complaint against another..."*

DAY 4: Ephesians 4:1-6 *"...bearing with one another in love..."*

DAY 5: 2 Corinthians 2:5-11 *"...forgive and comfort him..."*

DAY 6: 2 Corinthians 5:16-21 *"...be reconciled to God."*

DAY 7: Genesis 37:1-36, 45:1-15 *"...Joseph, whom you sold..."*

OBEY
Head: Think, *"What do I learn about God and people?"*

Heart: Ask, *"God, what are you saying to me today?"*

Hands: Decide, *"How will I respond to God's voice?"*

GOING DEEPER
* Who from your past has chosen to forgive you?
* Who do you need to ask God for help to graciously forgive?

34

DO NOT THROW YOUR PEARLS TO PIGS

READ MATTHEW 7:1-7
"*6* Do not give dogs what is holy, and do not throw your pearls before pigs, lest they trample them underfoot and turn to attack you."

While Jesus is the most influential person in history, people today, and 2,000 years ago, chose to reject his message. Even when hearing directly from Jesus, some people are unwilling or unable to receive spiritual truth! Likewise, despite our deep desire to communicate God's love to the world, we *will* encounter people who respond with disinterest, antagonism or even harm! Over-earnest Christians may be surprised to hear that the same Jesus who gave up His life for all humanity does not expect *us* to persist in conversations or relationships that are unproductive or harmful.

Taking Jesus' example of a pig, it's worth noting that Jesus' point isn't that we should treat people who reject Jesus as pigs. Rather, his point is that like a pig that chomps down a pearl, slop or steak without regard for its nutrition or value, some people devour God's spiritual truths along with pop psychology and social media. In fact, they may even value God's truths so poorly that they get angry with you for sharing them!

When we encounter people who are looking to "demolish" us or our message, we need to expect the outcome to endanger both ourselves and our message. In these instances, whether we are sharing the gospel or providing our best attempt at wise advice, we are best off engaging with them with dignity and saving our "pearls" for someone else who is willing to savour them.

This wisdom may not suit the over-earnest, soap-box Christians amongst us. However, it's important to observe that **Jesus didn't chase people, they chased Him.** While he calls us to take His message to the nations, he sees no need to subject ourselves to constant rejection and reproach. In fact, we see the practice of the earliest Christian missionaries (e.g. Paul in Acts 13:46; 18:6; 19:9) living out Jesus' instruction. These Christians often simply moved on if their offer of Jesus' gospel message was rejected! Likewise, we are called to be *followers* of Jesus not *pushers* of Jesus. There is no demand that we become over-earnest and unwisely persist with antagonistic or destructive people.

It may be that some people are explicitly called by God to

minister to people who are particularly antagonistic. However, this seems to be the exception, not the rule. While a desire to be a heroic missionary is noble, most of our lives, and much of the need is in the neighbourhoods, cities and workplaces that ordinary people like us live in. The reality is that not everyone in our neighbourhood is interested in Jesus, so we should feel free to find the ones who are!

Are you wasting time on people who aren't interested in God instead of those who are?

DAILY RHYTHM

PRAY
Centre your mind upon Jesus. Pray, "Come, Holy Spirit".

READ
Make time to read God's Word out loud each day.

DAY 1: Matt 7:6 *"...do not throw your pearls before pigs,..."*
DAY 2: Matthew 15:21-28 *"Have mercy on me, O Lord..."*
DAY 3: Proverbs 9:1-12 *"The fear of the Lord is the..."*
DAY 4: Ephesians 4:25-27 *"do not let the sun go down..."*
DAY 5: John 12:37-50 *"I did not come to judge the world..."*
DAY 6: Romans 11:1-12 *"But if it is by grace, it is no longer..."*
DAY 7: Proverbs 26:1-11 *"Answer not a fool according..."*

OBEY
Head: Think, *"What do I learn about God and people?"*
Heart: Ask, *"God, what are you saying to me today?"*
Hands: Decide, *"How will I respond to God's voice?"*

GOING DEEPER
* Are you trying to love or share Jesus with people who are simply disinterested or damaging?
* Is there someone in your life who is open to God and his love to whom you could reorient your time and energy?

35

DO UNTO OTHERS...

> **READ MATTHEW 7:12-14**
> **"¹² So whatever you wish that others would do to you, do also to them, for this is the Law and the Prophets.** ¹³ *Enter by the narrow gate. For the gate is wide and the way is easy that leads to destruction, and those who enter by it are many.* ¹⁴ *For the gate is narrow and the way is hard that leads to life, and those who find it are few."*

Our culture often restates this saying of Jesus as "do unto others as you would have them do to you". We call this command the Golden Rule because it's not just a summary of all of the Law and Prophets (the pre-Jesus part of the Bible) but Jesus says it *is* the Law and the Prophets. Put simply, relating to others as we would have them relate to us *is* a summary of every doctrine, teaching, command, poem, prayer and story in the Bible.

Significantly, the summary of God's revelation to mankind

isn't, "Thou shalt *not*" but rather, "Thou *shall*". While Jesus clearly affirms God's ongoing *negative* directives to avoid sin, "Do not get drunk", "Do not lie" and "Do not have sex with someone you're not married to", he summarises God's desire for humanity as a *positive* directive to love.

Today's world says if you can simply avoid doing "bad stuff" (e.g. "Don't be evil") then you are a "good" person. However, Jesus speaks of a higher way of living. A way in which we don't just avoid the Devil, but pursue Jesus - imitating God's design for humanity as modelled by Jesus.

Significantly, this pursuit of Jesus includes a willingness to love people regardless of the response we receive. Jesus didn't wait for us to reciprocate. His example guides us away from the passivity of the status quo to the brilliance of a life marked by proactive, no-strings-attached love for others.

Interestingly, Jesus clarifies that this kind of life is not a free-for-all, "do what feels good" kind of life. Rather, it's a life based on "the Law and the Prophets". Anyone who wants to live this kind of life needs to "enter by the narrow gate". In other words, he, not we, defines the way to this kind of, "Thou shalt" life. He makes it perfectly clear that while this kind of life is his perfect design, it's "hard"! The reason is simple; left to ourselves, our society does to others what suits ourselves. It takes God, his laws, Spirit and people to guide us to the narrow gate and the hard road that leads to life!

If there was ever a time when the world needed followers of

Jesus to take the hard road and live this kind of proactive life it is now. Jesus' "golden" strategy is the one that is most likely to truly set us free from our greatest limitation - ourselves.

In what way can you mirror God's love for others, treating others as you would like to be treated?

DAILY RHYTHM

PRAY
Centre your mind upon Jesus. Pray, "Come, Holy Spirit".

READ
Make time to read God's Word out loud each day.

DAY 1: Matthew 7:12 *"So whatever you wish that others…"*

DAY 2: Luke 6:27-36 *"…bless those who curse you…"*

DAY 3: Romans 13:8-10 *"Love does no wrong to a neighbour;"*

DAY 4: Galatians 5:13-26 *"…that you are not consumed…"*

DAY 5: 1 Corinthians 13:1-8 *"Love is patient and kind…"*

DAY 6: 1 Thessalonians 5:12-24 *"…help the weak, be patient…"*

DAY 7: Lamentations 3:22-23 *"…steadfast love of the Lord…"*

OBEY
Head: Think, *"What do I learn about God and people?"*
Heart: Ask, *"God, what are you saying to me today?"*
Hands: Decide, *"How will I respond to God's voice?"*

GOING DEEPER

* How many of your sins against God has he forgiven?

* Is there a sin perpetrated against you that you have thus far chosen not to forgive?

36

DON'T SEPARATE WHAT GOD JOINS

> READ MATTHEW 19:1-12
> "³ "Some Pharisees came and tried to trap him with this question: "Should a man be allowed to divorce his wife for just any reason?" ⁴ "Haven't you read the Scriptures?" Jesus replied. "They record that from the beginning 'God made them male and female.' " ⁵ And he said, "'This explains why a man leaves his father and mother and is joined to his wife, and the two are united into one.' ⁶ **Since they are no longer two but one, let no one split apart what God has joined together.**"" (NLT)

Jesus is openly affirming of traditional, Christian marriage. This not only includes the basic structure for marriage between one man and one woman but the divinely guided fusion of their two lives into "one flesh". This union creates a new entity made up of two separate individuals that

God personally joins together as "one".

However, if we look around at our own families and neighbourhoods, many of these once-happy unions are now torn apart. So, while God does the *joining*, it is fallible human beings who are responsible for the *dividing*.

Clearly, Jesus is speaking to husbands and wives, reminding them of his desire for them to honour not just each other, but the union God has created between them. However, we would be naive to think that the only people who can influence a marriage are the spouses who are in it! A thriving marriage requires not only the presence of other people willing to foster the union and invest in the individuals but also protection from anyone who would seek to "split apart what God has joined"!

If we're willing, we have an opportunity to heed Jesus' call to not only help married couples live out the unified expression God designed for them, but also to avoid being complicit in splitting them apart. While there are times when divorce may be a valid option, we may be an unwitting participant in a divorce in a number of ways. We could be a third party that actively breaks the marriage covenant. Alternatively, we could passively contribute to divorce by watching from the sidelines without being willing to intervene or encourage reconciliation.

As followers of Jesus, we need to honour this concept of "one-ness" as a picture of His design for not just marriage but community, family and church. We can shape our conversations to honour, rather than dishonour, our own spouses. Without hiding from the deep challenges of marriage, we can encourage the married couples around us to embrace God's design and pursue a thriving, intimate union despite the sacrifices required. Finally, for those who know God personally, we can be assured that he has united himself with us forever! It's from this place of union with God that we are able to promote the same with our spouse or for the married couples around us.

Is there a "one flesh" union that you are in or around that you celebrate and champion with God?

DAILY RHYTHM

PRAY
Centre your mind upon Jesus. Pray, "Come, Holy Spirit".

READ
Make time to read God's Word out loud each day.

DAY 1: Matthew 19:4-6 *"...let no one split apart what God..."* (NLT)

DAY 2: Hebrews 13:1-7 *"Let marriage be held in honour..."*

DAY 3: Ephesians 5:25-33 *"love your wives, as Christ..."*

DAY 4: Genesis 2:20-24 *"...a man shall hold fast to his wife..."*

DAY 5: Proverbs 31:10-31 *"...her husband also...praises her..."*

DAY 6: 1 John 4:7-21 *"...does not love does not know God..."*

DAY 7: Song of Solomon 8:6-7 *"...love is as strong as death..."*

OBEY
Head: Think, *"What do I learn about God and people?"*
Heart: Ask, *"God, what are you saying to me today?"*
Hands: Decide, *"How will I respond to God's voice?"*

GOING DEEPER

* What model of marriage did you grow up with?

* How can you honour the marriages of those around you?

* MARRIED PEOPLE: Ask God this week how you and your spouse can pursue his model for a healthy marriage.

37

LOVE ONE ANOTHER AS I LOVED YOU

> READ JOHN 13:31-38
> "*³⁴ A new commandment I give to you, that you love one another: just as I have loved you, you also are to love one another.* ³⁵ *By this all people will know that you are my disciples, if you have love for one another."*

When Jesus teaches us to love others it is always in the context of His personal love towards us and His historical sacrifice for us all.

If His love for us is a guide for our own lives of love, it's worth taking time to contemplate, "How has Jesus loved me?" For some, his forgiveness of their sin is what first comes to mind. Others are overwhelmed that Jesus has promised to be present with them in every situation. Take a few minutes now to write a list of the specific ways you believe he has loved you. If you have yet to meet Jesus or feel like he hasn't met your expectations, I'd encourage you to attempt even a short, tentative list of what you know to be good and true about Jesus.

Once you've compiled a list of how Jesus has loved you, compile a second list of what you have done to deserve His love. Take time to think it through. Once that's done, compare the lists. If you're like most of us, one list will be much longer than the other! Clearly, Christ has loved us in more ways than we loved him. When considering what we have done for him, even the most heroic Jesus-follower couldn't declare that they'd loved enough to *earn* or deserve Jesus' love.

Jesus' willingness to give us undeserved love isn't intended to simply humble us. Rather, his list is a visual guide for us to love others *just as* he has loved us.

As you aim to love others like Jesus models, you may be tempted to pause or give up entirely, when their reciprocity is lacking. In the same way that Jesus' love towards us is far greater than our love for him, we should expect that when we follow his example, the outcomes may be similar. We may compile a long list of loving actions to others while their reciprocal list remains quite short. You may even find yourself asking questions like, "Why bother continuing to love someone who ignores me?" Or, "They act like they deserve this! They're so ungrateful!"

While we should avoid situations where people reject us entirely or are actively mistreating us, it's entirely normal for a follower of Jesus to love others more than they are being loved in return. In fact, Jesus understands this practice of loving other followers disproportionately as central to his strategy of reaching every nation with his gospel message. He says that if we learn to love each other like him, "all people will know" who we belong to and why it is that we love so deeply.

When people observe how you interact with other Christians, do they sense your deep, God-given love for them? Do they see that you have been taught by Jesus how much God loves them?

DAILY RHYTHM

PRAY
Centre your mind upon Jesus. Pray, "Come, Holy Spirit".

READ
Make time to read God's Word out loud each day.

DAY 1: John 13:31-38 *"...just as I have loved you, you also..."*

DAY 2: John 3:16-21 *"For God so loved the world, that he..."*

DAY 3: John 14:15-31 *"You know him, for he dwells with you..."*

DAY 4: John 15:9-17 *"...that my joy may be in you,..."*

DAY 5: John 17 *"...that they may be one even as we are one..."*

DAY 6: John 21:1-23 *"Simon, son of John, do you love me..."*

DAY 7: Psalm 129:1-24 *"How precious to me are your..."*

OBEY
> **Head**: Think, *"What do I learn about God and people?"*
> **Heart**: Ask, *"God, what are you saying to me today?"*
> **Hands**: Decide, *"How will I respond to God's voice?"*

GOING DEEPER

* Have you ever sensed God's deep love for you? If so, describe what that was like.

* How have you sensed God's love flowing out of other Jesus followers in your life?

38

GO TO CHRISTIANS WHO OFFEND YOU

MATTHEW 18:10-20

15 "If your brother sins against you, go and tell him his fault, between you and him alone. If he listens to you, you have gained your brother. 16 But if he does not listen, take one or two others along with you, that every charge may be established by the evidence of two or three witnesses. 17 If he refuses to listen to them, tell it to the church. And if he refuses to listen even to the church, let him be to you as a Gentile and a tax collector... 20 For where two or three are gathered in my name, there am I among them."

If you've lived for a day with another Christian you'll know that even followers of Jesus - even the "best" ones - sin against each other. The question isn't *if*, but *when*. Given Jesus' constant reminders to love each other, it may come as a surprise that he teaches us in Matthew 18 that we are to "go" and tell them their fault. For Jesus, just like his 'great commission' to take his good news to the world, restoring relationships with those who sin against us is meant to be dealt with proactively. As a prelude to this teaching and an explanation for how important it is to, 'go', Jesus tells the "parable of the lost sheep", one of Jesus' most famous stories. In this parable, Jesus outlines that like a shepherd who has 100 sheep, but one goes missing, God's heart is to pursue anyone who wanders and becomes separated from him *and* his people. With this story as a backdrop, Jesus makes it clear that we are to do likewise! When there is conflict, separation, or even just a wandering, we are to pursue that person. The goal Jesus has for us isn't to simply "call them out" on their sin but to "call them back in" to relationship and family.

The last sentence in this passage, "For where two or three are gathered in my name, there am I among them" is critical to understanding why this should matter to us. This passage is usually quoted with a focus on an expectation that Jesus' presence is promised wherever "two or more" Christians gather. However, the context encourages us to remember how important it is for him to have *all* his "sheep" living together in harmony.

If our focus is merely expecting Jesus to be with *us*, we have missed the point. If Jesus is present wherever two or more are gathered, then we shouldn't want anyone to miss out! Rather, Jesus is calling our focus to those who are *not* present with us due to our unwillingness to restore our relationship with them. Furthermore, Jesus may even be hinting that 'if you value your own experience of me without sharing my heart for the "lost sheep" who are separated from you, then you may not know me as well as you think!'

Like a shepherd who has lost one of his precious sheep, Jesus calls us to, *"Go now! Lay out the fault that you may be restored as family. Remember, they are missing out on not just a relationship with you, but time with you in my presence"*. In short, don't keep the beauty and power of the Christian community to yourself. Jesus came for us all and desires us all to be *together* as one.

DAILY RHYTHM

PRAY
Centre your mind upon Jesus. Pray, "Come, Holy Spirit".

READ
Make time to read God's Word out loud each day.

DAY 1: Matthew 18:15-20 *"If your brother sins against you..."*
DAY 2: Galatians 6:1 *"...if anyone is caught in any..."*
DAY 3: Luke 15:1-7 *"Rejoice with me, for I have found my..."*
DAY 4: Luke 17:20-21 *"...behold, the kingdom of God is in..."*
DAY 5: Proverbs 19 *"...it is his glory to overlook an offence.."*
DAY 6: John 17 *"...that they may be one even as we are one,..."*
DAY 7: Ephesians 4:1-6 *"...eager to maintain the unity..."*

OBEY
Head: Think, *"What do I learn about God and people?"*
Heart: Ask, *"God, what are you saying to me today?"*
Hands: Decide, *"How will I respond to God's voice?"*

GOING DEEPER

* Below is Jesus' four-step process of restoring conflict. What are your reflections on his recommendations?

    1. *[If it's safe to do so]* Meet privately with those who've sinned against you and tell them their fault. *[If it is not safe to meet with them (e.g. abuse, crime), seek a trusted person who can guide you through an appropriate process.]*

    2. If the person does not listen, go again with one or two other followers of Jesus.

3. If the person still does not listen, speak to the church and they will go to them.

4. If the person still does not listen, assume they are not a Christian.

* *How might Jesus' presence amongst his people motivate you to repair relationships?*

PART 4

GOD'S MISSION FOR YOU

~

39

SEEK FIRST THE KINGDOM OF GOD

> READ MATTHEW 6:25-34
>
> *"Therefore do not be anxious, saying, 'What shall we eat?' or 'What shall we drink?' or 'What shall we wear?'* [32] *For the Gentiles seek after all these things, and your heavenly Father knows that you need them all.* [33] *But* **seek first the kingdom of God and his righteousness, and all these things will be added to you."**

Have you ever had a friend who fell "head-over-heels-in-love"? They suddenly seem to have a "skip in their step" and a permanent smile on their face. This is because they are completely focused on the pursuit of intimacy with their new flame. The world could be falling apart and they'd barely notice!

This single-minded focus that overpowers all other concerns is similar to the life that Jesus calls us to. As he wraps up his famous "Sermon on the Mount" (starting in Matthew chapter 5), Jesus directs our attention away from our natural inclination to worry about our daily, personal needs (which God promises to meet) towards God's desires for ourselves and the world around us.

We often fail to respond to this call because we accept the myth that worries and self-interest will benefit us. This is a lie. In fact, it's only when we entrust our own "kingdom" to God and focus on his kingdom that our life is transformed into what we always hoped it could. In Romans, the Apostle Paul sums up the difference between these two kingdoms: "For the Kingdom of God is not a matter of what we eat or drink [our daily concerns], but of living a life of goodness and peace and joy in the Holy Spirit." (Romans 14:17).

The path to experiencing this Kingdom is to recognise that we are easily occupied with our own kingdom. While it's not uncommon for a Christian to declare, "I love God with all my heart", it's quite common to find their daily and weekly priorities full of activities that exclusively build their own kingdom. As Jesus makes it clear, focusing on our own kingdom brings about anxiety about...our own kingdoms!

To counter this outcome, we could pay more attention to how we spend our days and weeks. Are there glimpses of us pursuing God's desires for our own life (again, read from Matthew chapter 5 to see Jesus' examples of what this looks like)? Does your schedule foster "a life of goodness and peace and joy in the Holy Spirit"?

Please take a few moments now to write down two separate lists. Focus the first list on ideas that would help you prioritise God's kingdom over yours. In your second list, focus on regular activities that you could potentially eliminate from your week in order to focus on the activities in your first list. Ask God for wisdom to know how to embrace your new schedule that seeks to put God first in how you spend your time and energy.

DAILY RHYTHM

PRAY
Centre your mind upon Jesus. Pray, "Come, Holy Spirit".

READ
Make time to read God's Word out loud each day.

DAY 1: Matthew 6:25-34 *"But seek first the kingdom..."*
DAY 2: Matthew 13:44-36 *"The kingdom of heaven is like..."*
DAY 3: Luke 13:18-20 *"What is the kingdom of God like?"*
DAY 4: Romans 12:1-2 *"...present your bodies as a living..."*
DAY 5: Romans 12:3-21 *"Having gifts that differ..."*
DAY 6: Titus 3:3-8 *"...who have believed in God may..."*
DAY 7: Joshua 24:14-24 *"But as for me and my house..."*

OBEY
Head: Think, *"What do I learn about God and people?"*
Heart: Ask, *"God, what are you saying to me today?"*
Hands: Decide, *"How will I respond to God's voice?"*

GOING DEEPER
* *Write a list of activities that prioritise God's kingdom over yours.*
* *As a **part** of a response to Romans 12:1-2, how could you make space in your week to introduce just one of these activities?*

40

BE WISE AS SERPENTS, INNOCENT AS DOVES

> READ MATTHEW 10:16-25
> "*16* *"Behold, I am sending you out as sheep in the midst of wolves, so be wise as serpents and innocent as doves."*

It's been said that Christians can sometimes be *so heavenly-minded that they are of no earthly use.*

On one hand, this can lead to naivety, neglecting to take life's dangers and challenges seriously, resulting in unnecessary suffering for everyone involved. Conversely, throughout history some Christians have felt so emboldened that they "have the truth" and "God is for us" that they sin by dethroning God and acting in the role of judge, jury and executioner in all areas of life. Knowing our capacity for both naivety and harm, Jesus calls us to learn to *slither* in wisdom and *glide* in innocence.

We must learn to *slither* because not everyone around us is as well-meaning as we like to assume. Thus, while we courageously live lives marked by love, we are nonetheless to use every bit of wisdom, skill and strength we have available to protect ourselves and those around us. This includes a strategic and circumspect approach to our relationships, business, finances, family and mission.

However, while we are to take on the "wisdom of the serpent", Jesus does not expect us to harm or intimidate those who oppose us. There are many people in this world who react with venom to any opponent. However, as we slither *through* obstacles and around opposition, at no time are we to be found guilty of malice in our hearts or harm with our hands. We are to glide over even the most challenging of circumstances as innocently as a dove.

We see this perfectly illustrated in both the life and death of Jesus. He navigated many complex social and theological challenges with incredible wisdom and yet never took advantage of these opportunities to harm anyone. Rather, we are to draw people to their best future - one united with their heavenly father.

Likewise, may we be willing to find a way to *slither* through conflict, traps and temptations while remaining committed to learning to *glide* over attack, judgment or criticism. Let's not be naive and sinful, but wise and innocent. Let's learn to slither and glide just like Jesus.

Is there a situation in which you need to ask God for wisdom and innocence?

DAILY RHYTHM

PRAY
Centre your mind upon Jesus. Pray, "Come, Holy Spirit".

READ
Make time to read God's Word out loud each day.

DAY 1: Matthew 10:16-23 "...*wise as serpents and innocent*..."

DAY 2: Romans 16:17-19 "...*watch out for those who cause*..."

DAY 3: Ephesians 5:8-20 "...*making the best use of the time*..."

DAY 4: Colossians 4:2-6 "*Let your speech always be*..."

DAY 5: James 3:13-18 "...*righteousness is sown in peace*..."

DAY 6: 1 Peter 2:11-17 "...*your conduct among the Gentiles*..."

DAY 7: Titus 2:7-8 "...*having nothing evil to say about us.*"

OBEY
Head: Think, "*What do I learn about God and people?*"
Heart: Ask, "*God, what are you saying to me today?*"
Hands: Decide, "*How will I respond to God's voice?*"

GOING DEEPER

* *Can you recall a situation where you've been treated poorly by someone you were genuinely trying to help?*

* *Is there a situation in which you need to ask God for wisdom and innocence?*

41

SHEPHERD OTHER FOLLOWERS OF JESUS

READ JOHN 21:15-19

"¹⁵ When they had finished breakfast, Jesus said to Simon Peter, "Simon, son of John, do you love me more than these [other disciples of Jesus]?" He said to him, "Yes, Lord; you know that I love you." He said to him, "Feed my lambs." ¹⁶ He said to him a second time, **"Simon, son of John, do you love me?"** He said to him, **"Yes, Lord; you know that I love you."** He said to him, **"Tend my sheep.""**

Some of humanity's greatest stories immortalise the significance of someone's *last words*. In the gospel of John, we read Jesus' direct, even bold, *last words* to Peter who was the first leader of the fledgling family we now call Christians.

After establishing that their relationship is founded upon love, Jesus, referring to the other disciples, directs Peter to "feed My lambs" and "tend my sheep" as an expression of this love. Though not always glamorous or popular, this role as a shepherding, servant leader of other followers of Jesus is the pre-eminent model for the church that came from leaders like Peter.

The earnestness with which Jesus instructed His friend shows that this role is incredibly significant in His mind. Jesus' command also indicates a simple, uncomfortable principle for even the most mature of His followers - every one of Jesus' sheep needs a shepherd! Despite the strengths within each of us, we are prone to wander and in need of a human shepherd to constantly guide us back to Jesus' path. Even in seasons where we are surrounded by a "great bunch of Christian friends", we often still need someone to guide us in critical moments when we're vulnerable to prey, sickness or wandering!

Even Christian shepherds, pastors and leaders, need their own shepherd. No matter how thorough the training and development they have gone through, every shepherd is also a sheep. Every pastor still needs their own pastor if they are to stay healthy. Every mature man or woman needs another man or woman to lovingly guide them to a life and faith that nourishes them as Jesus promised it would.

If you're not sure if your priority is to find a shepherd or to be one, Jesus' encouragement to Peter to "feed" the "lambs" and "tend" the "sheep" may offer a clue. It may be that Jesus is describing the different degrees of shepherding some need. Some followers are like lambs, they can't feed themselves and need constant care from a stable, mature shepherd. More mature followers need much less attention, simply to be "checked in on" as they continue to follow Jesus for the long haul.

Reflect on your own spiritual maturity. Are you in need of a Christian community or leader who can lovingly "shepherd" you? Or have you matured over some time and are ready to pray, "God, highlight any sheep around me that you are calling me to humbly shepherd?"

DAILY RHYTHM

PRAY
Centre your mind upon Jesus. Pray, "Come, Holy Spirit".

READ
Make time to read God's Word out loud each day.

DAY 1: John 21:15-19 *"Yes, Lord; you know that I love you."*

DAY 2: Galatians 6:1-10 *"...you who are spiritual should..."*

DAY 3: 1 Peter 5:1-5 *"...be subject to the elders."*

DAY 4: Hebrews 10:19-25 *"...let us consider how to stir up..."*

DAY 5: John 10:1-18 *"The good shepherd lays down his life..."*

DAY 6: Acts 20:25-31 *"...care for the church of God..."*

DAY 7: 1 Corinthians 4:14-21; 11:1 *"...Be imitators of me..."*

OBEY
Head: Think, *"What do I learn about God and people?"*
Heart: Ask, *"God, what are you saying to me today?"*
Hands: Decide, *"How will I respond to God's voice?"*

GOING DEEPER
* Has anyone ever "shepherded" you in a healthy way? If not, who could do that for you? Start by looking around you first. If there's no one obvious close by, pray and ask God to show you someone else.

* Is there anyone in your life that God may want you to help guide in their own life and faith?

42

ASK GOD TO SEND PEOPLE ON MISSION

READ MATTHEW 9:35-38

"^{37} Then he said to his disciples, "The harvest is plentiful, but the labourers are few; ^{38} therefore pray earnestly to the Lord of the harvest to send out labourers into his harvest.""

Every harvest season in regional Australia there are more fruit and vegetables ready to be picked than there are workers to pick it. While there are plenty of city-dwellers who are unemployed or experiencing financial strain, few venture out to reap the benefits of the annual harvest.

Likewise, there are entire Christian industries dedicated to promoting the 'ripe' opportunities to share the message of Jesus with entire people groups who have never heard the good news of his love. Unfortunately, there are many Christians seeking purpose for their lives who never consider the invitation of Jesus to be sent out into this huge 'harvest'.

There may be many reasons for this disconnect between our desire to make an impact in life and the opportunities that are available to us, but one of them is motivation. Jesus makes it clear that his motivation for the mission he is sending us on is compassion for their "harassed and helpless" state of being (verse 36).

How do we cultivate this kind of compassion which compels us to "go"? It's by learning to see people like Jesus saw them. It's by encountering the heart of God for people just like us around the world. While we were *once* lost, there are billions of people who are *still* lost. Jesus makes it very clear that this means not only a lack of belonging to God's family but an eternity without him and the life that he offers.

This is why Jesus offers a heartfelt call to pray that many would join him in his "harvest", welcoming many sheep into the eternally safe, secure arms of their heavenly father.

However, in his typically proactive approach, after asking his disciples to "pray about it", it seems he immediately gathered 12 of his closest disciples and sent them out into this harvest directly! It's hard to know what Jesus would say to people like you and me today, but it's very clear that while he clearly intended them to pray for "labourers" to go out into the harvest, he had no problem gathering those who were ready and sending them out!

Jesus invites us to pray for and join his harvest. Are there people in the world that you know are "lost"? Pray God will send someone to them. Ask God if he is sending you. No doubt there are people around you right now - neighbours, family, friends, colleagues, teammates - who are lost. Maybe you are the answer to someone else's prayer for them. Ask God how you might enter into his harvest. Take a bold risk on whatever response you sense from him.

DAILY RHYTHM

PRAY
Centre your mind upon Jesus. Pray, "Come, Holy Spirit".

READ
Make time to read God's Word out loud each day.

DAY 1: Matt 9:35-38 *"...pray earnestly to the Lord..."*

DAY 2: Acts 13:1-3 *"...they laid their hands on them and sent..."*

DAY 3: 2 Thessalonians 3:1-5 *"...that the word of the Lord..."*

DAY 4: Acts 4:1-31 *"...continued to speak the word of God."*

DAY 5: John 17:20-26 *"...for those who will believe in me..."*

DAY 6: Matthew 28:16-20 *"I am with you always..."*

DAY 7: Isaiah 6:8 *"Here I am! Send me."*

OBEY
Head: Think, *"What do I learn about God and people?"*
Heart: Ask, *"God, what are you saying to me today?"*
Hands: Decide, *"How will I respond to God's voice?"*

GOING DEEPER

* Were you once *"without a shepherd"*? If so, when did that change?

* Make a short list of people around you who don't know God. Think of something you can do for one of them this week to shepherd them closer to Jesus.

43

LEAD BY BEING A SERVANT

> READ MATTHEW 20:20-28
>
> "*[26] But among you it will be different. Whoever wants to be a leader among you must be your servant, [27] and whoever wants to be first among you must become your slave. [28] For even the Son of Man came not to be served but to serve others and to give his life as a ransom for many.*" (NLT)

Social media has highlighted something inherent within humans throughout history - many of us enjoy the spotlight and the power that comes with it! Despite the incredible challenges and sacrifices any leader must make, people of every generation throughout recorded history seem to have an inbuilt desire to be seen as "great" amongst their peers.

Even in churches and Christian conferences, it's all too common to see heroes fashioned out of self-made millionaires, authors and CEO's. The message seems to be that every man, woman, boy and girl should aspire to be an executive, thought leader or "influencer".

However, the reality is that this style of leadership is not going to be suitable for the breadth of personalities, work, skills and interests that we all have. Furthermore, if every one of us is a leader/boss/business owner then who is left to follow, manage or do the essential work?

The good news is that Jesus offers a type of leadership that every single one of us is capable of excelling in - servant leadership. This is a type of leadership that operates in a completely unique manner.

Jesus describes to his closest followers that the leadership they sought was one that *exercised authority over* others. However, Jesus was introducing them to a leadership style that *exercised humility alongside* others. This was not a belittling of our own selves, but an elevation of others. While our natural instinct is to control others - children, spouses, friends, teammates or colleagues - Jesus firmly believed, taught and modelled that to be considered a "hero" in His kingdom requires that we lift others up. Christians who lead anyone in any context should prioritise compassion for those they lead, not control.

Finally, we can be assured of the power of this counter-cultural leadership mindset when we see the outcomes. Jesus-like leadership has Jesus-like outcomes. When we lead like

Jesus we see fruit like Jesus saw. Love abounds, joy increases, peace reigns and people are valued and free. This is the fruit we need in our churches today. This is the fruit we need in homes, businesses non-profits, clubs and schools. This fruit is the kind that comes from the servant leadership modelled to us perfectly by Jesus Christ, the Son of God.

Who is the greatest servant leader you have known? In what way could you lead others by serving them?

DAILY RHYTHM

PRAY
Centre your mind upon Jesus. Pray, "Come, Holy Spirit".

READ
Make time to read God's Word out loud each day.

DAY 1: Matt 20:20-27 *"Whoever wants to be a leader..." (NLT)*

DAY 2: John 13:1-17 *"...began to wash the disciples' feet..."*

DAY 3: Philippians 2:1-11 *"...by taking the form of a servant..."*

DAY 4: Luke 24:22-27 *"...Christ should suffer these things...?"*

DAY 5: 1 Peter 5:1-11 *"Humble yourselves, therefore, under..."*

DAY 6: Mark 10:35-45 *"But whoever would be great..."*

DAY 7: Acts 20:17-38 *"...care for the church of God..."*

OBEY
Head: Think, *"What do I learn about God and people?"*
Heart: Ask, *"God, what are you saying to me today?"*
Hands: Decide, *"How will I respond to God's voice?"*

GOING DEEPER

* Who is the greatest servant leader you have known? List the ways they served others.

* How could you live out servant-leadership to those around you?

44

CHOOSE THE NARROW GATE

> READ MATTHEW 7:12-14
> "*[13] Enter by the narrow gate. For the gate is wide and the way is easy that leads to destruction, and those who enter by it are many. [14] For the gate is narrow and the way is hard that leads to life, and those who find it are few.*"

We live in a world where the majority of us have more choices than ever. In comparison to most of history, we even get a smorgasbord of options when it comes to religious belief. Into this buffet of belief, Jesus singles himself out as different to every other choice. While his immediate audience would have contrasted him with the pagan and Jewish religions, the same principle is clearly meant to apply to us today. From amongst Judaism, Islam, atheism and all manner of ancient and modern spiritual options, Jesus says only he is the "*narrow gate...that leads to life*".

This isn't simply a claim of superiority, but it also rubs against our primal nature that defaults to the wide gate - the way of options, customisation, and combination. Jesus makes it very clear that if you're on the more popular or prosperous paths, you have missed him. He is clear that his path is the one that the minority, not the majority are willing to choose. This doesn't seem to be just because his path is *hard*, but that it's *his* path.

Jesus isn't simply calling us to, "do hard things". Rather, he's calling us to one single "hard thing" - giving up our rights to comfort and self-determination by making a conscious choice to choose him and the path *he determines* for us. In Philippians 2:8 we read that Jesus is very familiar with this call and the great cost that comes with it, "And being found in human form, he [Jesus] humbled himself by becoming obedient to the point of death, even death on a cross." Far from being morbid, we need to remind ourselves, that it's this hard, narrow path that has transformed history and our world! In fact, without Jesus choosing humility, we wouldn't have access to Jesus and all that he promises us.

Jesus wants us to be assured that when we choose him, we get not only real *limits* but true *life*. Some of these limits will be very stark and costly (rejection, ridicule, persecution or worse), but like Jesus' path, the outcome is always life in its deepest sense. It seems that Jesus is indicating that if you are willing to choose the narrow gate you get a deeper life and eternity with him. If you choose the path of least resistance, the wide gate, you experience not only a shallower earthly life but eternity without him.

Jesus knows we are all prone to choose *the path of least resistance*. He is graciously urging us to choose him, his limits and the life he offers to all who seek it.

Is there a way in which you have chosen, or are choosing the wide path? What would you have to risk if you chose the narrow path of Jesus?

DAILY RHYTHM

PRAY
Centre your mind upon Jesus. Pray, "Come, Holy Spirit".

READ
Make time to read God's Word out loud each day.

DAY 1: Matthew 7:13-14 *"Enter by the narrow gate..."*

DAY 2: Romans 8:31-39 *"If God is for us, who can be..."*

DAY 3: Hebrews 11 *"...without faith it is impossible..."*

DAY 4: Philippians 3:4-14 *"...I have suffered the loss..."*

DAY 5: Hebrews 10:19-25 *"Let us hold fast the..."*

DAY 6: John 14:1-14 *"I am the way, and the truth..."*

DAY 7: Habakkuk 3:17-19 *"...yet I will rejoice..."*

OBEY
Head: Think, *"What do I learn about God and people?"*
Heart: Ask, *"God, what are you saying to me today?"*
Hands: Decide, *"How will I respond to God's voice?"*

GOING DEEPER

* Is there a way in which you have chosen, or are choosing the wide path?

* What would you have to risk if you chose the narrow path of Jesus?

45

REMEMBER ME IN THE LORD'S SUPPER

> READ LUKE 22:14-23
> "[19] *And he took bread, and when he had given thanks, he broke it and gave it to them, saying,* "**This is my body, which is given for you. Do this in remembrance of me.**" [20] *And likewise the cup after they had eaten, saying,* "*This cup that is poured out for you is the new covenant in my blood.*"

There have been innumerable movies in which one of the pivotal scenes includes two friends or lovers saying their final goodbyes, exchanging keepsakes and declaring they'll "always remember" each other. Likewise, Jesus asked his friends and followers to "remember" him via a keepsake, a gift, that we call "Communion" or the "Lord's Supper". This simple meal usually involves bread and wine (or a cracker and juice) representing his body and blood sacrificed in our place on the cross.

Jesus inaugurated this meal in the middle of a Jewish Passover meal, a celebration of Israel's *exodus* ("departure") from slavery by the hand of God. It would be normal for any one of the Israelites who were rescued by God to say, "I'll *never* forget what God has done for me!". However, as all of us know, our memories do fade and our minds get distracted by the circumstances of life. This is one reason God gave them a Passover meal, so that as often as they would share this meal they would force themselves to remember how God had rescued them from a life of slavery. Similarly, Jesus gave all those who would put their faith in him a meal to invite them to remember how, through faith in him, God has rescued them from a life of internal sin-slavery.

Jesus gave only two elements in his meal, bread and wine. While he said the bread, "*is* my body", when he declared that the wine, "*is* the new covenant in my blood" it became clear that these elements are physical representations of a deeper reality. This promised "new covenant" that Jesus' death has made possible is God's new agreement that all people who put their faith in Jesus' death will be saved. Unlike the Jewish Passover in which a lamb is sacrificed to spare them from destruction, *Jesus himself* is the *sacrificial lamb* whose death spares us from destruction and brings us eternal life. Unlike the lamb which was sacrificed at each Passover, Jesus' death was once-for-all-for-everyone. He died *once* to atone for *all* the sins of *anyone* who puts their faith in him. This death launches God's new covenant with mankind that the Lord's

Supper celebrates.

Unlike a contract, which is void if one party breaks their agreed terms, a biblical covenant (e.g. a marriage "covenant") sees each party keep their terms even if the other breaks theirs. Since God will not break his terms to forgive us of our sins, we take communion to celebrate that Jesus' sacrificial covenant has freed us from all punishment for any and all of our sins! However, the Lord's Supper is not only a celebration of what his physical body accomplished, but his promised spiritual presence *in* and *with* us too (John 14:23, Matthew 18:20)! Finally, similar to friends separated by great time or distance, we anticipate when we will one day be *physically* present with Jesus just like his disciples where over 2,000 years ago. Amazingly, it seems that Jesus also anticipates the day when *he* gets to be with *us*.

DAILY RHYTHM

PRAY
Centre your mind upon Jesus. Pray, "Come, Holy Spirit".

READ
Make time to read God's Word out loud each day.

DAY 1: Luke 22:7-38 *"This is my body...given for you."*

DAY 2: 1 Corinthians 11:17-34 *"...is my body, which is for you."*

DAY 3: 1 Corinthians 10:14-31 *"Because there is one bread..."*

DAY 4: John 6:35-40 *"whoever comes to me shall not hunger..."*

DAY 5: Hebrews 9:1-28 *"...how much more will the blood of..."*

DAY 6: Romans 8:1-4 *"...is therefore now no condemnation..."*

DAY 7: Revelation 19:6-9 *"Blessed are those who are called..."*

OBEY
Head: Think, *"What do I learn about God and people?"*
Heart: Ask, *"God, what are you saying to me today?"*
Hands: Decide, *"How will I respond to God's voice?"*

GOING DEEPER
* *How could such a simple meal help you remember Jesus?*
* *When you take the Lord's Supper, what can you anticipate about the time when you are reunited with Jesus and can share this simple meal with him?*

46

MAKE GOD'S HOUSE A PLACE OF PRAYER, NOT PROFIT

READ MARK 11:12-19; 24-25

"*¹⁷ And he was teaching them and saying to them, "Is it not written, '**My house shall be called a house of prayer for all the nations**'? But you have made it a den of robbers.*""

When people visit your house, how do they describe it? The "tidy" house, "crazy" house or "fun" house? Every house, family or group can be defined by the atmosphere someone experiences when they visit.

Jesus had a confrontational encounter in a Jewish temple (his 'house') that was supposedly dedicated to the worship of God. It only took a moment to realise hypocrisy was at large and rather than being a place of worship it had become a place of profit, not prayer; a place to work, not worship.

To make matters worse, the temple had a series of 'courts'

for Jewish men, Jewish women and then Gentiles (non-Jews). It was this Outer Court of the Gentiles that was made into a marketplace.

This situation sees Jesus turned into a holy rage. Since the temple was a place where God's presence was said to dwell, hijacking the temple for profit was a direct rebellion against God himself. Not only were the Jewish people no longer cherishing God's presence through prayer and worship, but the Gentile people who had travelled vast distances to Jerusalem were having their access to God's presence diminished as well!

For Jesus, access to God's presence was key. Jesus came so that the Holy Spirit, God's very presence, could dwell within us, his family, and his Church. (1 Corinthians 6:19).

In the early days of the internet, 1995-2000, internet cafes existed for those who didn't have the internet at home to come and 'get online' easily. In the 2020s and beyond, we have access to the internet wherever we go. Some of us even choose to avoid 'connected' devices like 'smart watches' so that we can have a few moments each day where we aren't connected to the internet!

Likewise, Jesus lived in a time when the presence of God was available in the Temple. However, he came to begin the fulfilment of the Jewish prophecies that one day God's presence would be available to all! As post-Jesus believers in God, the same challenge exists for us today as it did for the early religious Jews. We have a choice to disregard or cherish God's presence. He's not in a temple, he's in us! Similarly, we have a choice to disregard or cherish those around us who come seeking God's presence in us. It could be a person of a different culture, religion, background or ethnicity who you have little in common with. But Jesus makes it clear that we are to pray ("for the nations") that they too will come to know and cherish God's presence themselves. That's why he came. That's what he has called us to. To share the presence of God that we've been gifted with!

DAILY RHYTHM

PRAY
Centre your mind upon Jesus. Pray, "Come, Holy Spirit".

READ
Make time to read God's Word out loud each day.

DAY 1: Mark 11:12-18 *"...a house of prayer for all the nations."*

DAY 2: Luke 11:1-13 *"Lord, teach us to pray..."*

DAY 3: Acts 2:42-47 *"...they devoted themselves to...prayers."*

DAY 4: Acts 3:1-10 *"...up to the temple at the hour of prayer..."*

DAY 5: Acts 4:23-31 *"...had prayed, the place was shaken..."*

DAY 6: Acts 12:1-19 *"...earnest prayer for him was made..."*

DAY 7: Acts 16:13-15 *"...supposed there was a place of prayer..."*

OBEY
Head: Think, *"What do I learn about God and people?"*
Heart: Ask, *"God, what are you saying to me today?"*
Hands: Decide, *"How will I respond to God's voice?"*

GOING DEEPER
* Do you believe God's presence is dwelling within you?

* How could you incorporate Jesus' call to pray for people who are yet to follow Jesus?

47

BEWARE OF FALSE PROPHETS

READ MATTHEW 7:15-23

"¹⁵ *Beware of false prophets, who come to you in sheep's clothing but inwardly are ravenous wolves...* ²¹ *"Not everyone who says to me, 'Lord, Lord,' will enter the kingdom of heaven, but the one who does the will of my Father who is in heaven.* ²² *On that day many will say to me, 'Lord, Lord, did we not prophesy in your name, and cast out demons in your name, and do many mighty works in your name?'* ²³ *And then will I declare to them, 'I never knew you; depart from me, you workers of lawlessness.'*

Jesus doesn't give too many warnings, so when he does, we need to listen! This warning isn't of *any* person who claims to speak on behalf of God, but of people who *claim* to speak on behalf of God but are *intentionally fabricating their 'prophecies'* in order to devour others! Jesus offers some practical help in identifying the false prophets by contrasting the difference between those we should listen to and those whose words we should reject entirely.

Firstly, Jesus warns us against listening to people who verbally claim to follow him but do not live out the will of his (and our) heavenly father. Jesus both models obedience to our father and teaches that all true followers of him don't just speak well of Jesus, but similarly live their lives in obedience to their heavenly father.

Secondly, Jesus warns us against anyone who claims to obey God but doesn't actually *know* him as their father. Rather than doing *God's will* in God's name, false prophets do *their will* in God's name. This comes from them not actually knowing God personally. If they did, they wouldn't possibly waste time on their own passions at the expense of God's people. Jesus emphasises his warning by declaring that these people aren't only dangerous, but they are not in his kingdom at all. Rather, they are living in the kingdom of darkness.

Jesus is so confident of the intentions of false prophets that he calls them 'ravenous wolves'. This is not just for effect. Rather, Jesus says they're like a wolf who kills one sheep to take on its appearance so that it can ravenously attract and devour more sheep! Jesus isn't aiming to shelter you from new ideas, but from wolves who mimic Jesus in order to destroy his followers. The ravenous nature of these wolves has only one benefit, they eventually give away their true identity. If you observe a "wolf in sheep's clothing" long enough, you will see what the Bible calls the "fruit" of their life. Good fruit means they are a sheep. Bad fruit means they are a wolf.

To protect yourself, simply look for leaders who not only know Jesus but lead you to truly "know" him personally yourself. The more you get to *know* Jesus, the less likely you are to be tempted by the bait wolves set in order to devour you. While we have Christ, his teachings and his Holy Spirit as our primary guides in life and faith, take a few moments to consider if there is someone in your life who can lead you into a new intimacy with God.

DAILY RHYTHM

PRAY
Centre your mind upon Jesus. Pray, "Come, Holy Spirit".

READ
Make time to read God's Word out loud each day.

DAY 1: Matt 7:15-23 *"Beware of false prophets..."*

DAY 2: 1 John 4:1 *"Beloved,...test the spirits..."*

DAY 3: Acts 17:10–12 *"...examining the Scriptures daily..."*

DAY 4: 2 Peter 1:16-21 *"For no prophecy was ever produced..."*

DAY 5: 1 Corinthians 11:1 *"Be imitators of me, as I am..."*

DAY 6: 1 Timothy 3:1-13; *"...must be above reproach..."*

DAY 7: Titus 1:5-16 *"...are many who are insubordinate..."*

OBEY
Head: Think, *"What do I learn about God and people?"*
Heart: Ask, *"God, what are you saying to me today?"*
Hands: Decide, *"How will I respond to God's voice?"*

GOING DEEPER
* *Have you ever identified false prophets/leaders? How?*
* *Is there anyone in your life right now who is leading you further away from Christ?*

48

BEWARE OF FALSE TEACHING + RELIGION

READ MATTHEW 16:5-12

"*⁵ When the disciples reached the other side, they had forgotten to bring any bread. ⁶ Jesus said to them, **"Watch and beware of the leaven of the Pharisees and Sadducees."**...¹¹ How is it that you fail to understand that I did not speak about bread? Beware of the leaven of the Pharisees and Sadducees." ¹² Then they understood that he did not tell them to beware of the leaven of bread, but of the teaching of the Pharisees and Sadducees."*

Unless you're a baker, you may not know what 'leaven' is and why Jesus is talking about kitchen ingredients with his disciples. Leaven, was fermented dough from a previous batch of baking that was used in making new dough rise. Similarly, modern bakers use a very small amount of yeast to transform flat flour into the soft, fluffy loaves we love to eat.

For Jesus' illustration, the key characteristic of leaven is that only a small amount can transform a whole loaf. While in other teachings of Jesus, yeast is the heroic truth of Christ which permeates the whole loaf; in this story, the leaven is the villain who spoils the truth of Jesus. Put simply, while a hint of Jesus' truth can transform your life, a hint of lies can destroy it.

While this concept makes perfect sense to us, like the disciples, few of us stop to consider what lies could be diminishing the truth Jesus offers us. While the disciples found themselves worrying about their daily "bread" (our food, shelter and clothing), Jesus knew the greatest challenge ahead of them wasn't unleavened bread, but untainted truth.

History often reminds us that, "The pen is mightier than the sword". What we *believe* can conquer what no soldier could. And, like a double-bladed sword, the pen, can cut both ways. While the truth can set people and nations free, lies can, and still do, enslave individuals, families and nations. For some, their life has been derailed by a single sentence: "God couldn't love *you*". Some groups are told, "People like *you*, don't belong here." These lies can 'leaven' even the strongest of hearts.

Conspiracy Theories are still alive and well in the 2020s! While some seem increasingly plausible, others are simply magical thinking. However, no matter their validity, conspiracies have the power to overtake our lives. Everyone has met someone whose life and thoughts have been radically altered by a 'tainted' view of reality. A *tiny* conspiracy has "leavened" their *entire* worldview.

Have you added a lie, religious or otherwise, to Jesus' truth? Typically, lies revolve around religious striving or earthly comforts: "If you don't do *xyz*, you're not good enough for God", or, "If you aren't rich and healthy, God's upset with you". Whatever the lie, they can very easily steal the joy and freedom of knowing Jesus personally. Like Jesus taught the disciples, their greatest challenge is not bread but truth. If you add anything to Jesus, you don't have the simple freedom he offers.

DAILY RHYTHM

PRAY
Centre your mind upon Jesus. Pray, "Come, Holy Spirit".

READ
Make time to read God's Word out loud each day.

DAY 1: Matthew 16:5-12 *"...beware of...the teaching of..."*

DAY 2: Matthew 14:13-21; 15:32-39 *"...How many loaves..."*

DAY 3: 1 Corinthians 2:2 *"...nothing...except Jesus..."*

DAY 4: Galatians 3:1-9 *"Did you receive the Spirit by works..."*

DAY 5: Romans 2:8-9 *"it is the gift of God, not a result..."*

DAY 6: Romans 1:16-18 *"For I am not ashamed of the gospel..."*

DAY 7: John 14:25-29, 16:7-11 *"the Helper, the Holy Spirit..."*

OBEY
Head: Think, *"What do I learn about God and people?"*
Heart: Ask, *"God, what are you saying to me today?"*
Hands: Decide, *"How will I respond to God's voice?"*

GOING DEEPER
* What is the most impactful truth you've learnt from Jesus so far?
* Are any lies 'leavening' your life and faith in Jesus?

49

BE PREPARED FOR MY RETURN

READ MATTHEW 24:36-51

"*⁴² Therefore, stay awake, for you do not know on what day your Lord is coming. ⁴³ But know this, that if the master of the house had known in what part of the night the thief was coming, he would have stayed awake and would not have let his house be broken into. ⁴⁴ Therefore you also must be ready, for the Son of Man is coming at an hour you do not expect.*"

Modern Christians tend to focus on Jesus' entry into the world as a baby more than they do his promise to return as King. While Christmas is truly worth celebrating and a great time to share his message, Jesus himself calls us to ensure that we are "ready" for his return. Given how adamant he is, it's worth considering, "Exactly how do I get 'ready'?"

While we tend to think preparation involves learning, via

courses or books, if we read around Matthew chapters 24 and 25, Jesus gives us a few clues to getting ready.

Firstly, we are to be "awake" and "ready" for Him to return *at any time*, given that no one knows the day or hour to expect him. Secondly, this state of readiness is characterised by active anticipation, not a sleepy idleness. In Matthew 24 and 25, this action seems to be a matter of fulfilling the roles and tasks that God has called us to do in our own lives and to faithfully become the kinds of people that mirror the life and love of Jesus.

In a very simple way, this is like a parent asking their children to clean their room at the end of each day. "OK Guys, I'm going to cook dinner and when I come back I want everything to be perfectly in order!" Anyone who has made that request knows that the issue isn't that the average child will simply refuse to do their job but is most likely to either fight with a sibling or just get distracted! Like children, we need a reminder to "stay on target and stop mucking around!" We are easily distracted from not just our calling in life but also our identity - followers of Jesus called to live lives marked by love! So let's be "ready" for Jesus' return by doing the things, and being the people that, he has called us to!

Recently, my sister returned from a long period of living and working in a remote part of the world! We joined a throng of people in the lounge at the International Airport anxiously awaiting her return. While everyone in the lounge sat blankly, staring at their phones or pretending to be asleep, when *their* relative or friend came through the doors, they sprang to their feet and enthusiastically welcomed their loved ones.

When my sister came through the door the whole family likewise, jumped up, yelled out and ran to embrace her. This response is the kind of active anticipation for Jesus' return he is asking for! Being 'ready' for Jesus isn't being sound asleep thinking, "I'll see you when I see you", but, "I can't wait to see you, Jesus!" What would active anticipation of Jesus' return look like for you?

DAILY RHYTHM

PRAY
Centre your mind upon Jesus. Pray, "Come, Holy Spirit".

READ
Make time to read God's Word out loud each day.

DAY 1: Matthew 24:36-51 *"...for the Son of Man is coming..."*

DAY 2: Luke 12:35-40 *"Stay dressed for action and keep..."*

DAY 3: Titus 2:11-15 *"waiting for our blessed hope..."*

DAY 4: 1 Corinthians 15:35-58 *"we shall all be changed..."*

DAY 5: Mark 13:32-36 *"But concerning that day or..."*

DAY 6: 2 Corinthians 5:1-10 *"we have a building from God..."*

DAY 7: 1 Thessalonians 4:13-5:28 *"...like a thief in the night."*

OBEY
Head: Think, *"What do I learn about God and people?"*
Heart: Ask, *"God, what are you saying to me today?"*
Hands: Decide, *"How will I respond to God's voice?"*

GOING DEEPER
* Do you believe Jesus is "coming" again to earth?
* What would 'active anticipation' of Jesus' return look like in your life?

50

LAY UP TREASURES IN HEAVEN

> READ MATTHEW 6:19-24
>
> "[19] *"Do not lay up for yourselves treasures on earth, where moth and rust destroy and where thieves break in and steal,* [20] *but lay up for yourselves treasures in heaven, where neither moth nor rust destroys and where thieves do not break in and steal.* [21] **For where your treasure is, there your heart will be also."**

Have you ever visited a new friend and been given "the tour" of their house? It's not usually a way of showing off, but often a way of vulnerably sharing their life with you. Often the tour involves one special thing that your host is particularly proud of. It could be a car in a garage, a beautifully manicured lawn, a high school sports trophy, a new TV, a piece of art or simply their favourite book. Oftentimes this moment of pride is them revealing their most treasured possession to you. It's the item that has really captured their heart.

While Jesus isn't against cars, gardening, sports, technology, art or books, he reminds us that while everything on earth fades or fails, heaven's treasures are ours for eternity! It's not clear whether Jesus means *treasures that will last into our time in heaven* (love, joy, peace), or if he is referring to the *treasures in Heaven that he discusses elsewhere will be given as rewards* (heavenly 'crowns') to those who imitate Christ well on this earth (loving the unlovable, forgiving those who sin against us, sharing God's good news with those around us).

However, if we focus on the words "lay up", it seems that whatever Jesus is asking of us, it is very active, even obsessive! Maybe the closest illustration is to that of a treasure hunter, like the wild old Indiana Jones movie character. One thing you'll notice about each of those movies is that each movie involves only one treasure to be hunted down. That's because even Indiana Jones can't pursue *both* the Ark of the Covenant and the Holy Grail at the same time!

Similarly, Jesus makes it clear that it's impossible to treasure *both* God and money. We can treasure God and have money, but we cannot treasure money and have God. Every one of us will come to a point where we have to decide to hunt for either God's treasure or the worlds. It's not about being poor on earth, but rich in heaven. It's not about having no money, some money or a lot of money, but rather treasuring God above anything else we possess or pursue.

At the end of the day, the choice is ours. One love, God or

money, will rule the other. And the fearful but freeing decision Jesus gives to us is simply, "Choose your treasure". One of the greatest surprises for Christ-followers is that when you choose Jesus as your treasure, you discover a new level of freedom with your finances. Jesus actually shows you how to master money, rather than money mastering you. As is always the case with Jesus, his path is not just true, but beautiful, and life-giving! Are there any 'treasures' in your life that have captured your heart over and above God? Are there heavenly treasures that you need to grow an appetite for?

DAILY RHYTHM

PRAY
Centre your mind upon Jesus. Pray, "Come, Holy Spirit".

READ
Make time to read God's Word out loud each day.

DAY 1: Matthew 6:19-24 *"For where your treasure is..."*

DAY 2: 1 Timothy 6:3-20 *"...brought nothing into the world..."*

DAY 3: 1 Peter 1:3-25 *"...an inheritance that is imperishable..."*

DAY 4: Colossians 3:1-17 *"...have been raised with Christ..."*

DAY 5: Philippians 3:12-21 *"But our citizenship is in heaven..."*

DAY 6: Luke 12:22-34 *"Instead, seek his kingdom..."*

DAY 7: 2 Chronicles 16:9 *"...eyes of the Lord run to and fro..."*

OBEY
Head: Think, *"What do I learn about God and people?"*
Heart: Ask, *"God, what are you saying to me today?"*
Hands: Decide, *"How will I respond to God's voice?"*

GOING DEEPER
* *What treasures have you pursued in your life thus far?*
* *Are there heavenly treasures that you need to grow an appetite for?*

51

GO, MAKE, BAPTISE AND TEACH DISCIPLES

> READ MATTHEW 28:1-20; MARK 16:15
>
> "[19] *Go therefore and make disciples of all nations, baptising them in the name of the Father and of the Son and of the Holy Spirit,* [20] *teaching them to observe all that I have commanded you. And behold, I am with you always, to the end of the age.*"

When someone leaves this earth after a full life, we often say that they have left a good "legacy". Right before Jesus ascended into heaven he left more than a legacy; he left a directive that would transform history and eternity.

The directive, often called 'the Great Commission' essentially has four parts to it: "go" and "make disciples" by "baptising them" and "teaching them" to obey all His commands. In reality, this is simply a mirroring of what Jesus had done for His followers.

He had literally come down from heaven to find people who were looking for him. As people responded to his gospel message and invitation to, "come, follow me", he baptised them (though Jesus didn't baptise himself, he had his disciples do it. See John 4:1-2) and taught them to obey all that the Father had commanded him to teach.

Each of Jesus' followers is called to not only follow Jesus personally but to follow his example by giving the same invitation to every person, in every nation, on every continent, throughout the entire world. As we find people who want to become disciples (followers) of Jesus, we are to initiate them into their new life by baptism and continue to teach them how to live like him in every way we know!

It's sobering to realise that this rag-tag band of followers were not Ivy-league elites, but regular people. It's not only bewildering that Jesus believed that they were capable of fulfilling his directive, but also that **he likewise trusts regular people like you and I**! So rather than focusing on the enormity of the *task* he has given to us, I encourage you to reflect upon the enormity of the *trust* he has placed in us. This kind of divine trust doesn't just provide a sense of security but is meant to provide the kind of courage that propels us out of our limitations, comfort zones and habits into a future where we find ways to help others find and follow Jesus just like us.

As he trusts us to fulfil this mission, so we need to trust him to do what only he can do! As much as we'd like to 'make' people follow Jesus, none of us can manufacture true faith. Rather, we can simply point people to Jesus and trust the Holy Spirit, *Jesus'* spirit, to work miracles and transformation in their lives.

How do you feel knowing that God trusts you to fulfil his mission? What difference does it make to know Jesus has promised to be present with you wherever you go?

DAILY RHYTHM

PRAY
Centre your mind upon Jesus. Pray, "Come, Holy Spirit".

READ
Make time to read God's Word out loud each day.

DAY 1: Matthew 28:1-20 *"Go therefore and make disciples..."*

DAY 2: Romans 10:1-15 *"And how are they to believe in him..."*

DAY 3: Matthew 4:18-25 *"Follow me, and I will make you..."*

DAY 4: John 15 *"You did not choose me, but I chose you..."*

DAY 5: Luke 10:1-24 *"The harvest is plentiful, but the..."*

DAY 6: John 4:1-38 *"...the fields are white for harvest."*

DAY 7: Luke 24:46-47 *"...the forgiveness of sins...proclaimed..."*

OBEY
Head: Think, *"What do I learn about God and people?"*
Heart: Ask, *"God, what are you saying to me today?"*
Hands: Decide, *"How will I respond to God's voice?"*

GOING DEEPER
* What difference does it make to know Jesus has promised to be present with you wherever you go?

52

RECEIVE GOD'S POWER FOR MISSION

READ LUKE 24:36-53

"⁴⁴ Then he said to them, "These are my words that I spoke to you while I was still with you, that everything written about me in the Law of Moses and the Prophets and the Psalms must be fulfilled." ⁴⁵ Then he opened their minds to understand the Scriptures, ⁴⁶ and said to them, "Thus it is written, that the Christ should suffer and on the third day rise from the dead, ⁴⁷ and that repentance for the forgiveness of sins should be proclaimed in his name to all nations, beginning from Jerusalem. ⁴⁸ You are witnesses of these things. ⁴⁹ **And behold, I am sending the promise of my Father upon you. But stay in the city until you are clothed with power from on high.**""

It's remarkable that the ragged bunch of individuals who first followed Jesus had any impact upon the world at all. They were ordinary, competitive and sometimes even downright selfish.

Unsurprisingly, Jesus taught that their success in taking His "good news" beyond their homeland was not reliant upon their own strengths, skill sets, personalities or unique strategies. Rather, Jesus guided them to seek the power of God's Holy Spirit.

As with all of the teachings of Jesus, he never calls people to something that he has not pursued himself. His command to wait to receive God's power was simply an invitation to receive the same power that he also possessed.

Even though Jesus was sent from heaven by our Father, it wasn't until after he was baptised that he became "full of the Holy Spirit...[and] led by the Spirit" and living "in the power of the Spirit" (Luke 4:1,14). It wasn't until the Holy Spirit fully indwelled him that he began to publicly fulfil God's call upon his life. Likewise, if we are to do the *work of Jesus* then we need the *power of Jesus*. To fulfil the call God has for you, you need to be full of, led by and empowered with God's Holy Spirit just like Jesus!

This is not simply a nice idea. Rather, throughout history many people have had stories where they experienced a supernatural in-filling of God's Holy Spirit that transformed their life, faith and love forever. This new life and power can come at the moment of salvation or even days, weeks or years later. Whenever he comes, *you will know it!*

The first Christians heeded not only Jesus' example (Luke 4) but also his advice (Luke 24). At the beginning of the book of Acts, we see the disciples gathering in anticipation of Jesus' promised Holy Spirit. While they had no idea what would come of their waiting, when he came, *they knew it!*

If you cannot recall a season where you've been full of, led by or empowered by the Holy Spirit then ask for that today. Simply ask out loud for the Holy Spirit to fill you up. You might even want to repeatedly pray this simple phrase, "Come Holy Spirit".

DAILY RHYTHM

PRAY
Centre your mind upon Jesus. Pray, "Come, Holy Spirit".

READ
Make time to read God's Word out loud each day.

DAY 1: Luke 24:1-53 *"...stay in the city until you are..."*
DAY 2: John 14:5-21 *"...he will give you another Helper..."*
DAY 3: John 20:11-22 *"...[he] said..."Receive the Holy Spirit.""*
DAY 4: Acts 1:1-11 *"...you will be my witnesses..."*
DAY 5: Acts:2:1-21 *"...they were all filled with the Holy Spirit..."*
DAY 6: Ephesians 3:14-21 *"...with power through his Spirit..."*
DAY 7: Luke 4:1-4 *"And Jesus, full of the Holy Spirit..."*

OBEY
Head: Think, *"What do I learn about God and people?"*
Heart: Ask, *"God, what are you saying to me today?"*
Hands: Decide, *"How will I respond to God's voice?"*

GOING DEEPER
* *Have you ever had an encounter with God's Holy Spirit?*
* *Does knowing God's Spirit is with you change anything?*
* *If you don't sense God's presence with you, what could your next step be?*

WHAT NEXT?

We know from reading Jesus' words in the biblical books of Matthew, Mark, Luke and John that he expected those who *accepted his invitation* to "follow" him, literally *obeying His commands*. However, as we have seen throughout Jesus' teachings, his invitation isn't to a life of robotic duty, but a thriving spiritual life that starts with faith in his life, death and resurrection! If you are yet to put your faith in Jesus completely, revisit the first chapter, *Going All-In*.

Once you've gone "all-in", adopting the following three simple rhythms will help keep your faith thriving, not just surviving.

#1 GET TO KNOW JESUS

While this book has introduced you to Jesus' most basic commands, there is no limit to what you can discover in Jesus! Learning to pray, reading all of the gospels (the first four books of the New Testament that are all about Jesus) and then the rest of the Bible will provide a great foundation. Be prepared to discover new aspects of Jesus, and as you do, you'll notice Jesus will introduce you to new aspects of yourself! This process of discovery is endless.

#2 INVITE OTHER PEOPLE INTO YOUR LIFE

Jesus taught and modelled a life that lovingly welcomes others. Informally, Jesus showed us how to "do life" with those around us by sharing a meal like Jesus or opening up our calendar or home in other ways. Formally, you might start a group in a cafe or your home that encourages people to study the Bible and know Jesus themselves! Whatever the format of the invitation, learn to open your life like Jesus. As he so simply put it, learn to, "love your neighbour as yourself".

#3 GATHER TO ENCOURAGE OTHER FOLLOWERS

Jesus not only spent huge amounts of downtime with his friends and followers, he also modelled weekly gatherings with other Jewish believers to study God's Word, pray and worship together. His disciples, the first Christians, learnt from his example and not only spent time in each others' homes but also worshipped regularly together. Like every other area of life, following Jesus is best done together! No matter how fresh your faith is, you're designed to both receive and give spiritual encouragement! If there is no local church in your area, look for a small group of local Jesus followers to gather with each week. If that falls through, <u>find an online church today!</u> (www.churchathome.com.au)

If you can aim to develop these three rhythms you'll find that your faith can thrive through the many challenges of life!

The life you're designed for and Jesus promises isn't meant to be mediocre or mundane, but vibrant, giving us a taste of what eternity will be like with him.

If you've gone "all-in", then please, come, *follow Jesus* into life as it was designed to be.

CONTACT

As you follow Jesus, you will need the encouragement of other Christians! I'd encourage you to find a church, start a church or at least reach out to another follower of Jesus.

If you find yourself without someone to discuss faith in Jesus, please contact me!

Dan Harding
dan@openroad.church

To order more copies direct from the author please visit:
www.52follow.com

May our Lord Jesus Christ himself and God our Father, who loved us and by his grace gave us eternal encouragement and good hope, encourage your hearts and strengthen you in every good deed and word.

– 2ND THESSALONIANS 2:16-17

NOTES

NOTES

NOTES

NOTES

NOTES

NOTES

NOTES

NOTES

NOTES

NOTES

www.ingramcontent.com/pod-product-compliance
Lightning Source LLC
Chambersburg PA
CBHW011150290426
44109CB00025B/2550

* 9 7 8 0 6 4 8 6 1 0 7 2 4 *